WHEN KIDS KILL

Other books in the Virgin True Crime series

HV
9067
.H6
2003

WHEN KIDS KILL

Shocking Crimes of Lost Innocence

Jonathan Paul

SAUK VALLEY CC
LRC

First published in 2003 by

Virgin Books
Thames Wharf Studios
Rainville Rd
London W6 9HA

Copyright © Jonathan Paul, 2003

The right of Jonathan Paul to be identified as the Author of the Work
has been asserted by him in accordance with the Copyright, Designs
and Patents Act 1988.

This book is sold subject to the condition that it shall not,
by way of trade or otherwise, be lent, resold, hired out or otherwise
circulated without the publisher's prior written consent in any form of
binding or cover other than that in which it is published and without a
similar condition including this condition being imposed on the
subsequent purchaser.

ISBN 0 7535 0758 7

Typesetting by TW Typesetting, Plymouth, Devon

Printed and bound by Mackays of Chatham PLC

For Chris Ifould

CONTENTS

ACKNOWLEDGEMENTS

Dr Susan Bailey; Tim Bateman (NACRO); Mary Capner (*Chester Chronicle*); Joe Eames (*Caernarfon Herald*); Stan Gallagher (for sterling work on the rough edits); Ann Gallagher (for research); David Hovatter; Chris Ifould (for all his help and encouragement); James Marriott and Kerri Sharp; Nicola Tattersal (for Dr Bailey); Stephanie Williams, and Bernice Wolfenden.

Careful the things you say,
Children will listen.
Careful the things you do,
Children will see.
And learn.

Children will not obey,
But Children will listen.
Children will look to you
For which way to turn,
To learn what to be.

Careful before you say,
'Listen to me.'
Children will listen.

Stephen Sondheim,
Into The Woods

INTRODUCTION

Providence, USA: 1921. Three-year-old John and the little girl who had become his friend – also aged three – were thought to be safe enough, playing in the backyard: what harm could come to them? Then John put a cord around his playmate's neck. He tied the other end round a grindstone and turned the handle slowly but surely until his playmate was dead. When asked why he'd done this terrible thing, he replied, innocently enough: 'I don't like her any more.'[1]

He was, in the true sense of the word, 'innocent'. Learning about life includes learning about death. A boy who is cruel to insects, or who throws his teddy into the bathwater in order to drown it, is only playing 'What if . . .?' A girl who 'wishes her mother was dead' is merely discovering the difference between love and hate, and finding out that neither lasts forever. John from Providence was doing the same thing, but in his case the results would indeed last forever.

Children who are 'trouble'; who join together and become vicious; bullying that gets 'out of hand'; sadistic teenagers and homicidal toddlers – when they make the headlines it is seen as a ghastly aberration: an indication of social sickness. But could these horrific cases actually be explained another way? Do we too often forget how bewildering, how downright dangerous an experience childhood can actually be?

Miss Jean Brodie, Muriel Spark's charismatic school-mistress, said, 'Give me a girl of an impressionable age and she is mine for life.' According to Wordsworth, 'The child is the father of the Man', and, similarly, the Jesuits maintain that if you 'Give me the child; I will show you the man.'

To a child, the twenty years from birth to adulthood is like a long, long road. To those of us who are growing nearer to our final destination, we cover the same distance with what appears to be increasing speed: those two decades are no longer the seeming eternity that they used to be. We use our life experiences to map the way for our own children; their journey is made clearer by showing them our own mistakes. At least, that is what we would all like to believe.

Yet, for every generation of children and young adults, the way is far from clear. As parents, relatives, teachers or friends, or simply as members of society, we battle constantly to guide young minds towards what we see as right and healthy while at the same time trying to keep them from dangerous and damaging influences. Paradoxically it must be, to some extent, a losing battle: without an awareness of the darker side of life, children will grow to be vulnerable and ill-equipped adults. The consensus would maintain that there must be a balance; children need to be let off the lead gradually. Through the various danger points (the 'terrible twos': the pre-teens, puberty and adolescence), they will need adult reassurance, support and advice. There is no prescribed, 'success guaranteed' method of raising children. The best we can hope for is that we can pour as much good as possible into their lives and limit the harm we and others, inevitably, will do to them.

I recently appeared in a play in which, contrary to the famous advice that actors are given, I worked alongside a brattish child actor whose mother was constantly around rehearsals. The girl, who was about ten or eleven, was the stereotype personified: precocious, ill behaved, attention-seeking and with a piping voice which could be heard a mile off. Her mother, herself a frustrated actress, was equally archetypal: doting, over-protective and completely blind to the impression her little star was making on the rest of the company. This maternal indulgence was countered by fearsome chastisements if ever the girl didn't come up to the mark 'professionally'.

I confess to hating that child: we all did. She and her terrible mother were a favourite topic of conversation in the bar. The pair of them were perfect butts for our anger and malicious humour: they were quite obnoxious and any objective person would have sympathised with our attitude. Then, one evening, I forced myself to consider the girl as she actually was, rather than the mini-horror it was so easy to see her as. She was just a child who had been taught – trained – to behave in that way. Her inappropriate behaviour had always been rewarded – literally applauded – and her natural childishness was (again literally) always slapped down. She had, in effect, been created out of the frustrations and anxieties of her mother. It became starkly evident when one stopped disliking her sufficiently for the few seconds that it took to see it. As a colleague later observed: 'The poor kid didn't have a chance.'

Am I saying that all children's misdemeanours are the result of their parents' mistakes? No, I am not. There are very often other factors involved but, when considering the alarming and painful subject I am about to investigate, I wish to put away the notion that some children are 'born evil' or that violence of any kind is an aberration affecting only the relatively few whom it is easy to distinguish by it.

3

Children's innate cruelty does not usually extend to murder. Those who have, for whatever reason, killed other human beings before the age of eighteen (which seems to be a reasonable cut-off point between childhood and early adulthood), are generally notorious cases, regarded with ghoulish fascination by press and public alike. Naturally, there is a deal of genuine, laudable and entirely necessary concern: for the bereaved families, for the state of our society, and for the safety of other children. While it is understandable that the culprits are demonised and vilified, it is nevertheless regrettable that attempts to find reasons for their behaviour are greeted with howls of protest. Society seems always to prefer easy, if ill-informed, 'solutions' – 'lock 'em up and throw away the key'.

1. WHY KIDS KILL

Dr Susan Bailey OBE is a consultant adolescent forensic psychiatrist at the Bolton, Salford and Trafford Mental Health Partnership. She has been an expert witness in some of the cases I will cover in this book, including the trial of Robert Thompson and Jon Venables.* She is a likeable woman: quietly spoken and with an attractive northern accent. One can imagine that children would find it easy to like her and her professional competence is evident. We met in July 2002 and, although she was not able to comment on individual cases in which she had been involved, she answered my questions readily and spoke generally about her subject.**

Some children, she said, having begun life in deprived circumstances, experience disappointment and rejection. Unable to control the real world around them, they learn that being violent and difficult gives them the illusion of power. In some of the cases, particularly where the child is still at home, he or she can control and dominate their parents and, within the limited confines of their environment, this makes them almost all-powerful.

Because these children have been neglected and let down, they often find it very difficult to have any sense of self-worth. They find that doing things to hurt other people gives them a direction; it is a way of finding

* See 'The Killing of James Bulger'.
** The interview took place in London on 23/07/02.

self-fulfilment that they cannot get in any other way. It is also, in many cases, the one thing the child can do that it knows will provoke a reaction. Knowing that people are annoyed with you, afraid of you or even that they dislike you, is preferable to being ignored.

When they lack security, self-worth and love, children grow up with the feeling that life has little or nothing to offer them and that they are not going to achieve anything. They are let down at home; they are let down at school and they are let down in the community. They replace constructive self-awareness with self-preoccupation, constantly trying to discover what they are about: what they want from life and what they can do. Once they are set on this path, they (and Dr Bailey points out that this is not a large group but 'a small number who are actually like that') become totally self-obsessed. This self-obsession manifests itself not in a conscious way but, rather, in their persistence in doing damaging things in a subconscious attempt to fulfil their own needs. They have stopped thinking of and relating to other people in a normal way and regard not just any*thing*, but any*body*, in their lives as an object that is there to serve them.

Dr Bailey explains further:

> That's because they have usually had this profound rejection or abuse and they can see no sense of purpose. [Seeing people as objects] gives them a way of dealing with their life and a point in existing. These are the characteristics of some [problematic children] but by no means are they shared by all of them. However, it is this group who are more likely to be sadistic, the reason being that if you cease to see other people as other than objects, then being sadistic is not a difficult

leap to make: you're doing harm to an object, not to a person. It would seem this happens in the group of children who have experienced lots of inconsistency, lots of rejection and put-downs. There is no saving grace in their life; there is nothing that ever turns up trumps for them; everything goes wrong.

These can be typical 'problem kids' from deprived, difficult backgrounds, but not necessarily. Deprivation can also happen in what seem to be normal, materialistic homes, where it would appear that the children are given everything they could need and want – except, that is, emotional security.

There are theories about unwitting damage being done to babies when the parent (usually the mother) leaves the child alone for even a short time. When life experience is limited to a few weeks, a few minutes can seem like an age and anxieties can surface that remain with that child for the rest of its life. Dr Bailey was not sure whether this idea carries much weight. She thought it much more likely that children who commit 'grave crimes' have suffered from a more substantial dispossession:

I wouldn't stretch it to that point. Some people would say that but I think it's much more likely to be something tangible. These children haven't had as much emotional input as others. They may have had what is thought necessary: they've been cared for, they've been catered for – and some of them haven't – but there's nothing supporting them; there's nobody who has had any interest in them other than materially. They have been described as 'the lost boys' – and they are emotionally lost. Somebody may look at them and say:

7

'That's awful. They've not had a bad rearing; nobody's been dreadful to them . . .' However, they've had really very little emotional input. These groups tend to be socially isolated. They're the ones who would make friends with other children who are similar to themselves. These are the kinds of children who schoolmates would refer to and say, 'Well, yeah. He was with the nerdy group'. This is the group that has limited, fixed interests; the group that has to find somewhere to belong – and I'm referring now to the ones who have come from what we would class as better, more normal families.

Bullying is sometimes a factor. Quite often it is, at one and the same time, the reason for isolation and a response to it. It may be what could be described as 'straightforward' aggression from their peers. Although this is now targeted in schools as a policy requirement, there are cases where it goes unnoticed and may even be hidden from adults by the victims themselves. Where parents are concerned, the old advice is sometimes given: 'kick them back even harder and they'll leave you alone'. Dr Bailey maintains some victims consider it better to keep their problem to themselves rather than to tell somebody who then does nothing about it: 'They've plucked up the courage to say "I am being bullied", but then people are saying they've sorted it out when they patently haven't.' Sometimes the bullying is not so obvious: sometimes a child can be affected by the humiliating or disparaging approach of a particular teacher. Even petty cruelties may be magnified by the child on the receiving end and this can lead to violent retaliation, taking the form of self-harm, emotionally or physically, or a desire to harm others. Dr Bailey sees a correlation between children who have been humiliated in front of a class and those who go on to commit crimes with a sexual motive:

Whether that's right or wrong, that's their perception. It can be a trigger in the same way as when a child's anorexia may be a response to one key event. Maybe their boyfriend has said, 'Oh, you've put on a bit of weight' – it's quite often a casual comment – and that explodes in their minds and becomes the trigger to the eating disorder. There are instances where these children have had some very humiliating experiences: not the typical physical or sexual abuse, but what would constitute emotional abuse. When it happens at a time when they're particularly sensitive, the two things gel together and that sets them off on this isolated pursuit. A small number who go on to commit grave crimes begin with behavioural try-outs.

This 'behavioural try-out' starts when a child fantasises about harming people, not necessarily about killing them. They might have had thoughts about doing this before and they could even have made half-hearted attempts to put those thoughts into practice, but circumstances have pulled them back. Children learn to contain their baser instincts by first of all realising that bad behaviour causes displeasure in adults and then by a gradual understanding of their own conscience. When their lives spin totally out of control and these 'check and balances' are absent, they're more likely to give in to their compulsions. As Dr Bailey puts it:

Those who have thought about harming people previously are particularly boys with a sexual motive

whose victims are females of the same age or older.
They have imagined doing something and imagined
somebody else being involved.

The prototypes of those who rehearse their fantasies
can be found in American literature on adult killers
who have been reared in an isolated way. They often
have dominant mothers and research into their
background illustrates certain characteristics they may
well have in common. Quite a few of them have not had
particularly chaotic upbringings, but rather they come
from rigid, structured homes where there isn't a lot of
emotional warmth. There isn't this creature called a
'child killer'; he does not exist. It's a whole range of
circumstances and disorders.

A high proportion of teenagers break the law in some
way. Boys especially, often find themselves in trouble for
burglary or other types of robbery, such as mobile
phone theft. Whilst these crimes are not in any way
acceptable, they are often opportunistic and violence is
not the original motivation. Where a group of children
is involved, it is possible to find one among them who
views the experience differently to his or her companions. Most of the group have the sole intention of going
into a house to steal – often electrical goods that they
are able to sell easily to buy drugs or alcohol. One of
them may begin to quite enjoy going into the house and
will start to wonder if somebody is upstairs asleep:
'What would I do if they wake up?' Most burglars would
make themselves scarce – try not to get caught. This one
will flirt with the idea of discovery. He will stand over
the sleeping householder, not necessarily doing anything and not with any pre-conceived plan. He might
take keys or steal photographs. Later, he goes on to

think and plan, and then his behaviour becomes potentially dangerous.

The question must be asked: why do some children take their fantasies one step further and turn them into catastrophic reality? Part of the answer, according to Dr Bailey, is serendipity: circumstance – or, as she puts it more simply, 'bad luck'. She explains that there may be a layer of truth in the idea that if similar, unfortunate circumstances converged we might all be capable of doing similar things. Also, she continues, some may be fortunate enough to have protective influences that rescue them from the brink of disaster. For example, such a child may come into contact with a teacher or youth leader with whom, for some reason or other, they develop a particularly good relationship. This person spends time with the youngster and diverts them into, say, a sporting activity. The would-be offender is then taken along a different, more positive path. However, she points out that there will always be those who, even though they are on a more constructive course, remain solitary. These are the planners and 'seekers' who are still liable to become involved in criminal activity. If one were to ask their friends, they would maintain that that person was always, in some way, 'different' from the rest of them. Where other young criminals might round off an evening's thieving by going down to the pub or using drugs, this one would go off on his or her own. 'Odd' behaviour can often be an indication of distress or latent aggression.

Of course, there are cases where the child killer is simply acting on impulse: he felt the need to carry a knife and eventually he used it. This could be the case with quite a lot of children who are overactive, aggressive and compulsive. With escalating numbers of children – some of them very young indeed – becoming addicted to drugs, the potential for one of them to kill while 'under the influence' or desperate to get their next 'hit' is always there.

Sometimes, a few children with what could be termed 'unhelpful skills' band together. They pool these skills to catastrophic effect. That is to say, one may be good at robbery; one might be well practised at intimidating people; another is able to influence the others into taking drugs or binging on alcohol; and one in the group is severely disturbed and has sadistic ideas which he has so far kept to himself. If that mixture comes together, what could have been a 'normal' domestic burglary may well end up as a killing.

When such a group comes together, as happened with the murder on Hungerford Bridge (see Chapter 6), the effects of adrenalin can often take over and carry each along a road none of them would have necessarily contemplated individually. Dr Bailey also cites cases in America where normal high-school kids find distasteful websites and gradually descend into an inner world of fantasy in which they become totally absorbed. Whether on their own or with other children, they spend the vast majority of their waking hours, including most of the night and most of the weekend, completely immersed in these images, which begin to appear to be real. It takes a leader – an organiser – and a follower to come together and, once this has happened, imagined deeds can be put into practice in the real world.

There is, of course, a great deal of debate about the plethora of violent and overtly sexual images that are available to children. Even the most careful parent is unable to protect their offspring from them totally and some would argue that it would be wrong to do so. A child who is shielded from the world will grow up less able to cope with it when he or she eventually has to. On the other hand, a child who has become inured to violence may well be desensitised to its horror and its effects on others. Matthew Hardman did not need another person to spur him on to achieving his ambition to be a vampire and, through this, to take a human life. If websites and imagery could be responsible for such warped views of the world, did Dr Bailey believe that we should take urgent steps against them?

Suppose you are somebody who is vulnerable. Suppose, for instance, you've witnessed violence from a very early age: you've heard Dad leathering Mum – or Mum leathering Dad – or you've seen it, you've had the in vivo experience: the real life experience. Suppose then you are left in a situation where you're not particularly supervised and you can watch anything you want from morning till night and it's what you watch all the time. Then, yes, I think that does have an impact. Whether we want to do anything about it as a society, I don't know. But it is relevant.

However, there will be some things that might be harmful to some and might not be harmful to others. I don't just mean violent images: there's the cannabis debate, for example. There is a group of young offenders who abuse cannabis heavily: they get extremely paranoid and act on their paranoia. Conversely, the happy-go-lucky, well-adjusted adolescent who is experimenting may well just get chilled out. What do we do? Do we bring in legislation that always goes towards the group who are more vulnerable or do we not? That must be society's decision but, certainly, yes, visual imagery does have an impact. One has to say: 'What else does this child's life consist of?' If it consists of an uninspiring school career – not being very bright, not finding anything rewarding – then going home and sitting in front of some visual image – whatever that may be – and that's it, that's their whole experience, then how should we expect them to behave?'

This issue of the availability of extreme images is a popular one and it attracts a full range of opinion. At one extreme there are those who sincerely believe that even cartoon violence is harmful; at the other there are those who don't think second-hand experience of whatever type is going to have much effect. There are more considered arguments that take into account the readily available images on the news or on documentaries and make a distinction between these and the more gratuitous gore of, say, *Scream* or *Silence of the Lambs*. It could be said that the latter depiction of violence is less harmful simply because it is so extreme: children know that it isn't real; in the same way, they realise that the cartoon mouse who survives an exploding bomb would not be so lucky in real life. In fact, it is almost certainly the case, as Dr Bailey suggests, that reactions and resulting damage will depend very much on the child and on their experiences. Taking a toy gun away from a small boy is not going to ensure that he has a respect for life, and leaving it available to him is not necessarily going to turn him into a callous or dangerous adult.

What to other people might seem minor could be far more important to children: the loss of some treasured object; a friend who falls out with them; or an unintended put-down. To a young mind that has not yet learned to evaluate the relative importance of one thing against another, these issues are magnified and may cause explosions of anger. In those cases where the child is fixed, obsessive or where there are other contributory factors, these can be dangerous. For instance, a young boy in north London was recently stabbed to death by another after – so the reports state – an argument about football. Of course this murder is utterly senseless to a rational person, but the young assailant had grown up on a filthy, drug-infested estate where his sense of himself relied purely on his superiority in the pecking order of the local thugs. With this in mind, it seems surprising that these tragedies don't happen more often.

Children do not necessarily understand right and wrong in the way that we adults do. As we grow older, we develop the ability to put ourselves in the shoes of another person and to understand the consequences of our actions in terms of their feelings: to 'do as you would be done by'. Dr Bailey says this is quite a sophisticated capacity to have:

> Some children have never been given a sense of right and wrong; in others, it's acute. The normal thing about children is, it's about 'me'. Parents put boundaries round that and gradually the child learns and internalises it. But, at the very least, he or she would have to have a sense of permanence. You can find that some very bright, empathic children would know that when Mum says: 'Granny's gone to heaven', she doesn't mean that Granny's gone to somewhere where she can float back down again. She means: 'That's it! Granny's gone!' Others would not have this capacity: it's something that is very variable. This sense of permanence is one of the basic things I would look for

in determining the child's ability to distinguish right from wrong.

The question of how far a child can distinguish between these two precepts stands at the centre of many of the juvenile cases that go before courts all over the world. It becomes highly controversial in cases such as the murder of James Bulger, where the public and a bereaved family feel the killers have 'got away with it' as a result of their youth. On the other hand, if one considers the historic case of Jessie Harding Pomeroy,* who spent most of his life imprisoned for crimes he committed when he was a young teenager, the alternative can seem just as contentious.

If eighteen years of age can be regarded as the end of childhood, at what age can a child be held responsible for their actions, particularly of a criminal or violent nature? In most countries, limits are set: the age of ten in England, for instance. However, some ten-year-olds do not have the capacity for criminality at all, and some do. At the moment, the authorities who work with juvenile offenders are trying to develop more systematic and structured means of assessing that capacity; they are attempting to do this in ways that ten-year-old children are able to relate to. One such means is to show a series of pictures or scenarios to the offender and then talk with her or him, in child-friendly language, about cause and effect: 'If A does that to B, then B's not going to be very happy, and this is what it's going to mean for B and B's family'. Such an approach involves a lot of painstaking work.

Youth offender teams would typically carry this out with youngsters who have committed crimes that have

---

* See 'As Time Goes By . . .'

traumatised their victims: those who, for example, have been involved with burglary or assault. This is typical behavioural therapy, based on victim empathy, but it does not carry with it any guarantee of success.

Even if we are to believe that, to a certain level, children have an understanding of what is right and what is wrong, consider the circumstance where two or more children commit an offence, or where one or more adults are also involved. There may have been no premeditated intent and matters may, like Topsy, have 'just grown'. At what point can it be established that A was leading B? Or B leading C? At what point did those involved just get swept along by events? Where did the responsibility lie? This dilemma lies at the heart of the case involving the King brothers, who were accused of battering their father to death with a baseball bat.*

We hope that our own children, having gone through their adolescence, come out with an ability to recognise right from wrong and to understand and accept responsibility; these are good predictors that they might make reasonable adults and parents. Parents, teachers and others who have been involved in their upbringing will attempt to give them certain skills, which may be taught directly – arising out of ways of dealing with various situations that come up – or may be learned at second hand through, for instance, sports and games. Often such concepts and understandings will develop slowly, and what is learned or experienced in one context is not always applied or seen as relevant in another. When children are taken away from what is familiar – from their family, friends or home – their responses change very rapidly. Put them in foster care, a children's home

---

* See 'Blood Brothers'.

or a police station and the way that they behave can become totally opposed to how they behaved before. They may show understanding in a one-to-one interview but, if you put them in a distracting situation with a lot going on, then that understanding can go altogether. Particularly with younger children, knowledge and understanding is often situation-specific and not readily brought to bear in unfamiliar or upsetting circumstances. Some children have the ability to hold on to a moral stance by the age of ten and some haven't.

The Swiss child psychologist, Jean Piaget, observed children's learning and identified four stages in its development. These stages are normally worked through sequentially, although this is not always the case. The youngest children learn by 'doing' and are getting to grips with their senses: their ability simply, for instance, to touch or hold; to move towards or away from people or objects. Next they make their own sense of what they see around them, learning and behaving in a very egocentric way. They believe, for example, that the sun and moon follow them around and that, when they can no longer be seen, they have actually ceased to exist. Next they believe and learn only from what they can experience directly: what is concrete. Finally, they develop the ability to apply what they know in different situations from those where they were first learned and to have a logical approach that can be applied abstractly to wherever they happen to be and whatever they happen to be doing.

Young children are renowned for experimenting. In researching this book, I interviewed a man who, as a toddler, was discovered piling earth into the pram where his baby brother was sleeping. His mother saved the child from suffocation in the nick of time. When asked why he'd done it, the boy said that he'd seen his father planting bulbs. His father had said he wanted the bulbs to grow and so he was covering them in soil. The boy wanted his brother to grow so he did exactly the same thing.

Dr Bailey refers to a case in Norway where a child wanted to try out artificial resuscitation and, in order to test it, had to have somebody who needed it. So he had to put the person in a position where they *did* need it. This was a child at the 'concrete' stage, not sufficiently well developed to think about the emotional and other considerations. It was merely something to be tried out.

Dr Bailey continued:

It then takes a long time to say [to the child] 'Well, actually there's another way of looking at this, do you realise that?' And depending on what their experiences are, they may or may not realise it. That's the problem with looking at this subject. We're bound to have a law that says there's an age of criminal responsibility because, if we do it the other way and say we should assess them developmentally, that means that every child would have to be looked at and such an approach would require a huge work force; every case would be argued and the law would get very messy. I can understand why we have an age of criminal responsibility; I'm not sure it's the right age, but that is difficult.

Piaget, and other child psychologists who have followed and developed his work, would concur that most 'normal' children have developed the capacity to be held responsible for their actions by the age of ten, but as he and Dr Bailey acknowledge, this is a stage, is not age-related, and will not apply to all children. Of course, where killing has been proven, we are not talking about children from 'normal' backgrounds. From her own experience, Dr Bailey surmises that: '. . . a few children are just so badly abused themselves that they very rapidly take on the perpetrator's role in order to survive. They have the most awful role models, and they just go ahead and do similar things . . .'

Children play, and whether they're aggressive and cruel or not, will depend on which adults are there and whether they are saying: 'Think about what you have just done: what do you think that means to the other child?' They need to have guidelines; they need responsible adults, or sometimes older children, to show them boundaries. It is important to remember that they do not naturally find these limits for themselves. Some children who are impulsive go out to be much more bullying and aggressive in their play. They have little awareness of their behaviour and need help early on: they need someone to say, 'Hang on, what are you doing here? Just think about it.'

This is further compounded by what has been described as 'childhood lost': the idea that the years of innocence are getting fewer and fewer, and that the time-span of childhood has collapsed. Dr Bailey concurs from her experience: '. . . if you're lucky, they're still a child when they're eight; if not, they're pseudo-adults.' With so many examples to influence impressionable and powerless children, it is hardly surprising that the vulnerable and exploited among them take on the adult role models presented to them at ever earlier ages. If children are not getting early guidance and support from home (and for those most at risk, it is often parents and siblings who are the main abusers), this also limits the time for detecting and dealing with bullying and other anti-social behaviours. It means putting increasing pressure and responsibility on those at playschool and nursery to make early interventions to benefit children's personal, social and emotional development, and on schools to trigger behavioural and welfare support.

Through play and conversation, children also push the limits to find out how far they can go. It is not unusual for them knowingly to commit minor misdeeds in order to provoke a response that helps them sequence those actions or attitudes into their developing scale of social responsibility and acceptability. Equally, it is not unusual for a child 'not to know what they don't know' when faced with a world of fresh experiences and opportunities. A child may genuinely not know that they are doing wrong. If a child is not responsible for small misdemeanours, can it be culpable when there has been a murder? Dr Bailey:

> They may not be. That's why each case is seen on its own merits and dealt with in whichever way it is. Some children are found unfit to plead. This, in the case of a juvenile, may well be outside the remit of the standard reasons for an adult being found unfit – such as when they have a profound mental illness. A child may, at the time of the offence, have been hearing voices, or they have such a level of mental impairment they wouldn't know which day of the week it was.

The matter of how young offenders are dealt with in courts has recently brought the English legal system into conflict with European legislation, and even the United Nations Charter on Children's Rights. Dr Bailey continued:

Most cases have problems and difficulties. I think the way we deal with them is another issue and I think most children who go into secure care need what they get when they get there: containment boundaries, treatment, education, help to get on track again with their families. Then the movement into adult prison is seen as unhelpful and I wouldn't disagree with that. I think in the future the Youth Justice Board might be able to create something better in young offender institutions. I think the thing that is happening now is that those children wouldn't necessarily go from secure care into the run-of-the-mill institutions: they'd go into more specialised facilities for young offenders. So, I think it's like everything else: we learn the lessons and it takes us five or ten years to put it into practice.

The stage where we're at now is that some of the ones on longer sentences, when they hit the age where they can be classed as adult, are not just going into any old facility. They're going into more specialist units where, obviously, it's not the same as being in local authority care but certainly the treatment, the intervention and the way that the programme is delivered is as similar as it can be to what they had in secure care.

It may be possible to get two children from identical backgrounds – from the same family – one of whom goes 'wrong' and one who doesn't; or a child like Robert Thompson, who comes from a large family and turns out to be the one who has killed while the others haven't. The 'nature versus nurture' debate continues today, just as it always has done. According to the tabloid press, recent criminal cases involving juveniles can be explained by a mixture of the two: the child has a 'bad' or 'evil' nature and has grown up in unfortunate circumstances. While the notion that violent behaviour is a direct response to deprivation or abuse will not gain much sympathy, the idea that a child is inherently wicked, though far less likely, is a more popular one. Is a child's character formed entirely by their experience and background or is there a 'badness' in some that, at some stage, they will demonstrate no matter what? If nurture is responsible, why do some children suffer adversity and triumph over it? Dr Bailey's view is that:

. . . they've got their individual characteristics, they've got the adversity and the protective factors. But protection doesn't always come along at convenient times; it just happens at any time. So in the same family, the children may have all had the same adversity; but there may be a protective factor comes along – too late for one of them and just the right time for the other. One of them has his ears open and is receptive, but the other one's gone past that . . . it's what we call 'multiple gates': things that are positive and protective. It's no use just thinking that if we give them those protective factors it will all be all right. It will depend on what stage that child's at in their development as to what sort of impact it's having.

If you think about it, the child's on a path and there are things that are coming along that will make it worse all the time and there are sometimes things that will come along and protect them. And it's timing: that's the difficult one. You can have a child you're very worried about but the timing isn't right for the intervention for lots of reasons. They may not engage. You may know, because of other factors in the family, that they are not going to engage. When they're ready, *the waiting list to be seen might have stretched for miles. So all these things interact all the way along.*

Not only is it difficult to identify what causes may lead to a child becoming a killer, but it is also difficult to gauge when to intervene in their cure. The question of recognising the stage, the symptoms, the indicators, and of making the offer and the intervention at the right time is crucial. The lack of indicative behaviours in some children who go on to offend in the most extreme ways also presents society – and those who work with young children – with great challenges. In some young people, outward displays of aggression and emotion show something of the troubles that lie beneath, but this is not always the case. There are not always clear means of identifying those children who are under the kinds of influence and pressure that may lead to trouble.

Dr Bailey agreed that some children internalise their anger and some externalise it but that, while both of these approaches are possible, they can change. One thing we should consider is that children who externalise will, once in a blue moon, internalise. When this happens they are more likely to self-harm or even to be driven to suicide. Conversely children who internalise – who are very rigid, fixed, obsessional and who don't seem to have done anything aggressive – when they do have their little explosion, as Dr Bailey puts it, they 'do it for England'. All these things are on continuums.

What she looks for is pervasiveness: how much it invades all of their lives; the frequency and severity of when the child is 'ringing alarm bells'. When children do this very often, to a high degree, and behaviour indicative of stress is a major part of their expression, somebody may well read the signals and intervene.

Though the ability to put out such warnings will save some children, it is always possible to overlook them in others.

A child who has killed has deeply and irrevocably traumatised somebody else – the victim's family – but the killer is also traumatised. Children who have killed won't ever be the same again: there is evidence that trauma actually affects a person biologically. It is not only emotional damage that they need help for – their experience can also have a physical effect on their brain. Some of the children who have been abused, and then go on to abuse others, show evidence of post-traumatic stress disorder. Evidence for this has come from children who have been reared in a war zone. Nature and nurture are interlocking all the time.

Dr Bailey sees the need to look at change over time and to look at the variables. She feels that there is an obsession with risk assessment, but thinks that risk assessment has to go alongside needs assessment. This does not mean giving in to the children, but rather seeing what they actually need across the board. She is convinced that if you do that, and you are systematic about it, then you may drop the risk of some of these children becoming killers.

SAUK VALLEY CC
LRC

2. AS TIME GOES BY . . .

Delinquency, especially in its more extreme manifestations in the young, is often thought of as a product of our modern age. It may be a little fanciful to believe in a bygone period in which all children were obedient and respectful but, if pressed, many people would say that things are worse now. One may look for extenuating circumstances that affected youthful miscreants in times long gone (e.g. poverty, poor education, the bad influence of others), but these are excuses that don't seem to be viable with regard to today's delinquents. Yet we must consider that the passage of time dilutes public revulsion: works of fiction have bathed many vile deeds in a falsely romantic light and real-life 'exploits' that, if perpetrated in our own day, would be seen as monstrous, have been transformed by time into the stuff of entertainment. (The Artful Dodger, in reality, would have been a violent little thug, and Lizzie Borden giving her father and mother 'forty whacks' is sick material indeed to turn into an amusing rhyme.)

I am indebted to John Marr, of the wryly-titled and darkly humorous magazine *Murder Can Be Fun*, who has kindly allowed me to use his research for much of this chapter.[1] He lists several historic cases that are similar to the more recent tragedies documented in the pages of this book. He has also collected a chilling list of one-liners, all from the mouths of children who have killed:

'They were floating about like two drowned puppies.'
  – William Wild, thirteen, referring to his
    drowning of two toddlers, England, 1835
'Ain't dead yet? I'll make you dead.'
  – Hattie, nine, while hitting a two-year-old with
    an axe in retaliation for having been bitten by
    the infant, circa 1896
'So I could see the fire engines role!'
  – Thomas L, fifteen, explaining why he'd started
    fires in ten Manhattan apartment buildings,
    1925
*'I did not try to rob the Dobrindts, for what do I care
for the two or three years more you are able to give?'*
  – 'Cry Baby Bandit' Karl Muller, fifteen, denying
    that he had robbed a family of three he had
    murdered, Germany, 1927
'. . . Because she would not let me go to the picture show.'
  – boy's reason for shooting and killing his
    stepmother, Fort Myers, Florida, 1940
'I won't do it again.'
  – Welsh boy, nine, after drowning a
    four-year-old boy, 1947
*'I took the pram from outside the shop. There was a
baby in the pram and I threw it in the water. I just
wanted to do it.'*
  – English boy, nine, 1947
'I hated to kill but I had to. I'm insane.'
  – note left by fourteen-year-old Ohio boy who
    had shot his father, circa 1957
*'If I killed one they would just send me to reform
schools again but if I killed them both they'll send me to
the chair.'*
  – fourteen-year-old boy explaining why he had
    to kill two playmates, Arkansas, 1960

'Murder isn't that bad. We all die sometime.'
  – Mary Bell, eleven, 1968

HANNAH

The cry of innocent blood hath entered into the ears of the LORD of Sabaoth; but this day will silent [sic] its claims. Yes; in a few hours, will be executed the fatal, the tremendous sentence which puts a period to the life of one, who had never learned to live. In the beginning of life, a murderer.

So said Henry Channing in a sermon that was intended to make sense of the execution of a twelve-year-old girl. He went on:

Yes; my brethren, this poor prisoner, when committed to gaol, appeared to have no higher principle than the pleasure of gratifying her ungoverned passions. And so far from having the fear of GOD in her eyes – Oh tell it not in Gath! – she hath repeatedly declared to me, that she did not know that there was a GOD before she was told it after her imprisonment.

For, the ear of the children of men, being fully set in them to do evil, they hearken not, nor incline their ear. We have loved pleasures, and after them will we go.

. . . those under our care should be early inspired with sentiments which will raise them superior to irregular desires, and fleshy lusts which war against the soul. These too often like a strong man armed take captive the unguarded Youth, and lead him to the strange woman, whose house is the way to hell, going down to the chambers of death.

It is a relief to know that the ardent Mr Channing has been dead himself for almost 230 years. We are going back to the year 1774, to Groton, Connecticut, where Hannah Occuish had the misfortune to be born. Her parents were a frequently absent alcoholic Pequot Indian woman and a white man who had vanished completely, no doubt as soon as he heard the news of his daughter's birth.

At the age of six, in the company of her eight-year-old brother, she accosted another small girl. The brother and sister beat the child mercilessly, stealing her clothes and tearing a gold locket from around her neck. With their victim lying in a pool of blood by their feet, they then began to argue about how they should divide what they had stolen. Fortunately for the girl, she managed to raise enough consciousness to escape from her tormentors and report them to the authorities.

It was decided that the mother's influence was to blame for this unwarranted display of precocious violence. The children were removed from her 'care' and placed with other families. Her brother's fate was not recorded; Hannah went on to become the unpaid servant of the various people into whose charge she was given. Unsurprisingly, she grew into a resentful, malicious young girl to whom 'Theft and lying were . . . common vices'. In 1786, at the age of twelve, she was living outside New London, Connecticut, at the home of a widow. Though there are no reports of her employer being dissatisfied with her work or demeanour, the neighbourhood children were all 'very much afraid of her'.

Summer came and with it a healthy crop of strawberries, ripe for gathering. Eunice Bolles, who was only six, had a full basket; Hannah decided it would be easier to take the younger girl's harvest than pick her own. She stole them (presumably by intimidating the younger child but possibly by more surreptitious means). Eunice was dismayed and immediately went and told an adult. Hannah was duly punished and the matter could – and should – have ended there.

It was because of this trivial matter that Hannah ended up as the subject of Mr Channing's moralistic tirade. She wasn't about to let the little girl who'd told on her get away with it. Her revenge was premeditated, although it was, perhaps, somewhat hasty. About five weeks after the strawberries incident, Hannah saw Eunice on the way to school. Seizing her opportunity – and showing, in her actions, a capacity for quick thinking – she took an attractive piece of calico from the widow's house and a rock from the garden. Using the cloth as bait, and concealing the stone behind her back, she approached Eunice in a seemingly friendly manner, and smilingly offered to make up her quarrel. She showed Eunice the cloth, and perhaps offered to give it to her. Eunice was temporarily taken aback and not sure whether to trust the bully or not. She hesitated long enough for Hannah to inflict a terrible revenge.

Hannah brought the rock down on Eunice's head and kept on doing this until the child was a mass of blood, torn flesh and broken bones. Thinking her horrendous task accomplished, Hannah was about to leave when Eunice stirred. Hannah strangled the last vestiges of life from the mangled body, then piled rocks from a nearby wall on top of the remains. The intention was not to conceal the corpse, but to make Eunice's death look like an accident – a consequence of the wall's collapse.

The body was found soon enough and Hannah, along with others, was interrogated about the matter. She made up a story about four boys who, she said, she'd seen in her mistress's garden. She had shouted at them and they had fled. She said that soon afterwards, she had heard the sound of stones falling . . .

It was obvious that the death had not been accidental, for there was evidence of strangulation. Hannah, however, had given the investigators four fictitious suspects to pursue, and they had no immediate reason to suspect that she was lying. After a search for the boys proved fruitless and it became evident that no one else could report having seen them, suspicions were aroused and Hannah's 'helpful' statement made her the most likely suspect. She was taken to Eunice's crushed body, then awaiting burial, and confronted with what she had done. She broke down and confessed almost at once.

She was tried as any murderer would be, but with no concessions to the fact of her tender years. The case was a particularly unpleasant matter for all concerned and it was reported that even the judge was much affected by it. Those that witnessed the proceedings were revolted by the idea of so young a child being on trial for her life, but the law had no other provision for dealing with such a horrendous case and justice had to be seen to be done. Hannah, it is said, was probably one of the few people who did not seem to be undergoing any sort of emotional turmoil during the trial. Like some children of more recent times who have found themselves in front of a jury, she showed no signs of trauma and didn't seem to be overly concerned with what was being deliberated in court. She was found guilty.

In his summing up, the judge said: '. . . you must consider and realise it, that after death you must undergo another trial infinitely more solemn and awful than what you have passed through, before that God against whom you offended – at whose bar the deceased child will appear as a swift witness against you.' He went on: '. . . the sparing of you, on account of your age, would . . . be of dangerous consequences to the public, by holding up an idea that children might commit such atrocious acts with impunity.'

At first Hannah was, naturally enough, terrified, but she found comfort when she was told she would almost certainly be reprieved. Almost up to the date of her execution, she held on to this notion. Two weeks before she was due to hang, she realised the truth.

It was less than five months after the murder that Hannah Occuish was taken from the jail to a scaffold that had been erected in front of the meeting-house. There Mr Channing, a Yale minister, delivered his hour-long sermon to her and to the crowd:

> . . . Appetites and passions unrestrained in childhood, become furious in youth and endure dishonour, disease, and untimely death . . . But if you are not yet alarmed for your helpless offspring . . . go into our streets and . . . behold on every side children unrestrained practising iniquity with greediness. Children that have but just learned to speak are heard lisping forth horrid oaths and impious curses. We have here a striking evidence of the depravity of human nature; that we are indeed transgressors from the womb.

His diatribe ended, he turned to the terrified child they were about to hang and said to her: 'Hannah, the time for you to die is come. You will soon see that there is a great God who is angry with the wicked every day and will punish forever those whose sins are not pardoned before they die. If he is not more merciful than you, your soul cannot be saved. He sees nothing in you but wickedness: a poor wicked creature covered with the innocent blood of a helpless child crying to you for mercy.'

Hannah, at twelve years and nine months, was the youngest female ever executed in the United States (though a boy of ten was sent to the gallows in Louisiana, in September 1859. His crime is not recorded).

JESSE

The story of Jesse Harding Pomeroy is remarkable both for the sadistic viciousness he enjoyed meting out to other, smaller, children and for the resulting lifetime of state-sanctioned cruelty that was his punishment. No doubt there are some today, as there certainly were then, who hold that a killer – especially one who kills purely for his or her own gratification – should be treated as harshly as possible no matter how young they are when they commit their crime. One can picture the 69-year-old Pomeroy on his first transfer from one prison to another as he prepared to take his first proper* ride in a motor vehicle, blinking in the light of a strange, 'modern' outside world: a world from which he had been removed in his early teens. It's difficult to connect the pathetic old man with the heartless boy he had been so long, long ago. At that stage in his life he had spent 53 years in prison – no less than 41 of them in solitary confinement.

What sort of person had he become by then and what sort of child had he really been?

Jesse Pomeroy was born in Charlestown, Massachusetts, on 29 November 1859, the second child of a

---

* He had previously been taken for a drive once around the prison yard.

seamstress and a labourer. His father was later to change his profession and become a butcher but it is unlikely that Jesse was desensitised to viscera and gore because of this. As a child, he had suffered from what the Victorians called a 'humour' – some infection of what was then believed to be the fluid that controlled mood-swings. The first seven months of his life were a worrying time for his parents. Jesse did eventually recover, though he remained thin and sickly. His illness left him with a distinctive spot in his right eye. It didn't seem to affect him in any way, but it was noticeable and made him instantly identifiable. There are those who describe him as also having a harelip, but no reliable sources have mentioned this and, according to John Marr, it would be safe to put this detail down to over-zealous journalism. This desire to create a sensation could well account for the doubtful account of his having stabbed a cat and thrown it into a river when he was only a toddler.

He was a solitary child. He didn't seem to have any friends and spent most of his time with his nose in books. He particularly liked cheap cowboy-and-Indian novels such as those published by Beadle and Munro. One of his boyhood heroes was Simon Girty, whose adventures with the Shawnee Indians were based on a genuine figure of history, a white man who fought with Indians. Marr astutely points out that Jesse Pomeroy's crimes were not very far removed from the barbarous practices he would have read about in the more lurid descriptions of what the Indian 'savages' did to their enemies.

His schooldays were uneventful and his academic progress was average. His teachers thought him 'peculiar, intractable, not bad, but difficult to understand'. He had difficulty accepting criticism and was outraged whenever he was punished, whether he had deserved it or not.

At the age of twelve, he contracted pneumonia. Then, as now, it was an extremely serious illness and he could easily have died from it. At times, he was delirious and his mother noticed that he was never quite the same afterwards.

Indeed he wasn't: at the age of twelve he changed from being that poorly, rather isolated child, into a monster. It was Christmas 1871, and in Chelsea, a suburb of Boston that lay just across the river from where Jesse lived, a young boy was found unconscious. He didn't know the identity of his attacker, but when he described what had happened to him the town was horrified. The victim reported that a boy, older than he was, had taken him up to a lonely spot called Powder House Hill. Once there, he'd been forced to remove all his clothes and he'd been tied up. The older boy had then flogged him with a rope. This was not just an extreme case of bullying. The whole thing had been unprovoked; the attack had been formalised and so vicious that the child had eventually blacked out from the pain. On that occasion, the culprit was not caught.

Then it happened again – and again. In all, there were four victims, all of them about seven years old. The violence didn't always stop at flogging, either: they were cut with a knife and pierced with pins. The boy would humiliate his victims, making them say vulgarities such as 'kiss my ass'. He would scar their faces – especially round the eyes – as well as cutting their legs and genitals. He apparently derived great pleasure from what he was doing: they all described him as smiling all the time and laughing at their suffering.

It was a matter that had to be dealt with and the City offered a $1000 reward for information leading to the capture of the assailant. Known bullies were hauled in for questioning and paraded before the victims. None of them were identified as the culprit.

Then, seven months after they began, the attacks ceased.

Jesse's father had deserted his wife. Mrs Pomeroy was now facing the prospect of bringing up her two sons on a greatly reduced income. As a seamstress, she had at least the means of retaining a modest respectability, and she didn't intend to allow her misfortune totally to overwhelm her. She moved to South Boston and there set up a dressmaking business in rented premises. She was able to move her family into a flat directly opposite the shop at 327 Broadway. Her sons assisted her in the business and Jesse's brother Charles managed also to find employment, selling newspapers. Jesse, meanwhile, was spending his spare time terrorising the neighbourhood.

Harry Austin was eight years old. Jesse promised him money if he accompanied him to a nearby railway bridge. Once they were there – just as before – Jesse ordered Harry to strip. He tied him up and cut his body all over with a pocket-knife. When he was found, Harry had wounds under his shoulder blades and in one of his armpits, and his penis had been 'nearly half cut off'.

George Pratt was told he could have ten cents if he carried some newspapers for Jesse. He refused the job, but was willing to go with the older boy to the beach, where he was taken on board a yacht. The following statement is allegedly in George's own words. It is not couched in the language of a seven-year-old and is, therefore, likely to be a paraphrase of his story, which he signed as being a true account:

He said I had told three lies and that he was going to lick [beat] me three times. He told me to strip. I did not want to. He told me I must, so I did. He took a strap he had around him and hit me on the stomach and head. He paused between blows. He hit me fifty times, stuck a pin in my face, meddled with my private parts and stuck a pin in them. He put his hands over my mouth, threw me down on the floor and bit me on the cheek and back and right in the rump. He smiled while he was doing it. Then he told me to dress and go to sleep and he jumped out of the boat and disappeared.'

Joseph Kennedy, seven, was also offered money. This time it was to be in return for carrying a letter. He was taken to a boathouse where . . . (here we have, once again, what may be a paraphrase of what were taken to be his actual words):

He beat my head against the boathouse . . . He said if I hollered he would kill me. He stabbed me and scratched my hand with a horseshoe. Then he took me out onto the railroad. He had a big knife. He cut me in the face, three times on each side. Then he cut me here, made me say my prayers and naughty words and said he was going to kill me, that I never would see my father and mother any more.

Lastly there was Robert Gould, who was only five. He was taken to the railway where, just like the others, he was forced to take his clothes off. He was tied to a telegraph pole, his face was cut and he was flogged.

There are discrepancies as to the order in which these assaults came, but we do know that a few days after Robert Gould had been injured, Joseph Kennedy walked out of the local police station and recognised Jesse as he passed by on the street.

Pomeroy was arrested instantly. He denied any involvement in the assaults, even when other victims said he was the one who had hurt them: '. . . those boys that had been so maltreated by another came and said that I was the boy that did it to them and the only way they identified me was because I had a spot on the right eye.'

Johnny Balch was brought over from Chelsea. He also made a positive identification. The police had the evidence they needed and Jesse was accordingly sent for trial.

Jesse's mother was the one person who was to stand by him throughout. Though it's not really credible that she believed in his innocence, she always said she did. It is reasonable to assume that she found the prospect of having to come to terms with being the mother of such a perverted son too much to contemplate. Whatever her real reasons, in court she testified to Jessie's dutiful, obedient character. He had never been cruel to animals, she said (as had been suggested by one of her neighbours) – certainly not to other children – and the whole thing was utterly unbelievable.

Jesse was obviously guilty, but the court thought he was too young to fully appreciate how serious his crimes were. His lack of remorse – indeed, of any emotion at all – was seen as verification of this, and he was sent to a 'House of Reformation' for 'the duration of his minority'.

As if to justify his mother's glowing testament to his good character, Jesse showed his jailers nothing but virtue. He behaved well and impressed them as a decent, hard-working boy who had genuinely reformed.

Their trust in him was reflected in the privileges he was given, which eventually went as far as his having the free run of the school. Just one year into his sentence, his mother petitioned for his early release. Given that Jesse had worked so hard to improve and that he would be being returned to a stable, respectable family environment, the authorities agreed that there was no good reason to continue Jesse's incarceration.

He was released in February 1874 at the age of fourteen and everyone assumed that, having learned his lesson, he would now go on to lead a normal life. However, his sadistic urges had not gone away and it was only a few weeks before he indulged them again. This time he didn't stop at injuring his victim: this time it was murder.

It had always been boys that he had hurt before, so when nine-year-old Katie Curran vanished, Jesse wasn't considered to be a serious suspect. Another child claimed to have seen Katie getting into a buggy with a stranger and though the police did interview Jesse (along with everybody else in the area), they eventually concluded that she had been abducted by an adult. What had happened to the little girl might never have come to light had Jesse not gone on to kill again.

At the end of April, two young lads were playing on some marshland when they found the body of a small boy. The body was still warm and whoever had killed him had been especially vicious. Four-year-old Horace Millen had been mutilated from head to foot. His right eye was clotted with congealing blood from a stab wound and his body bore the marks of well over three hundred more cuts. His throat had been slashed right across and his genitals had been cut so badly that when the corpse was moved, his testicles fell onto the ground.

The killer had not made much of an attempt to cover his tracks. A trail of footprints was enough to tell the police that, incredibly enough, they were looking for another child. This was confirmed when they followed the trail to a wharf and there found witnesses, who said that Horace had gone off in the company of another boy.

It was immediately evident, when Jesse was questioned, that he was the killer. He had not cleaned the blood off his knife or his clothing. His boots still had mud on them from the marsh. He was shown Horace's body and asked 'Did you do this?'

He replied, 'I suppose so.' He went on to retract this half-hearted confession and thereafter always maintained his innocence. His mother, who must have been in emotional turmoil, took his side once again. This time it wasn't going to be so easy either to rescue him or to maintain her respectability and her livelihood as a shopkeeper: the murder had revolted everyone for miles around and, unsurprisingly, her dressmaking business foundered. Mrs Pomeroy was forced to let the shop go a month after Jesse had been taken into custody. The premises were taken by a grocery business next door and workmen moved in to start converting it. They couldn't help but notice a terrible stench emanating from the cellar. They assumed that it was caused by rats or some other vermin, just as the police had done some time before when they had searched the place for evidence relating to Katie Curran's disappearance.

Meanwhile, somewhat incredibly, Jesse had been asking his jailers whether there was any reward offered for locating Katie's body. What he had in mind isn't exactly clear, since he must have known there would be little chance of his collecting any money, even though he was the only one who knew where she was.

At the end of July, a builder converting Mrs Pomeroy's former dressmaking shop pulled at what appeared to be a scrap of material protruding from a mound of rubbish. He discovered that it was, in fact, a child's dress. He dug around a bit more and Katie's decomposing head was uncovered.

As before, Jesse said he had nothing to do with the little girl's death. His mother and brother were also arrested – possibly as much for their own protection as anything else, as their neighbours might have been ready to lynch them. Jesse didn't seem to be overly worried by the discovery, but was quick to point out that he didn't think his mother was guilty of killing Katie.

The truth – or, at least, a version of it – came out later (Jesse didn't tell the whole story: he would not confess to the excesses of cruelty he had evidently indulged in. The body was severely disfigured with knife wounds, just as Horace's had been). He said that Katie had come into the shop and asked if they sold 'school cards': 'I told her there was a store downstairs . . . I followed her, put my left arm about her neck, my hand over her mouth and, with my knife in my right hand, cut her throat. I then dragged her behind the water closet . . . and put some stones and ashes on the body.'

He was fastidious about the details and corrected an officer who had written 'in the cellar' when he had said 'downstairs': 'I didn't say "cellar", I said "stairs", for if I had said "cellar" she wouldn't have gone down.'

He still couldn't give any reasons for his terrible actions. Asked why he'd killed the children he said, 'I do not know. I couldn't help it.' He then pointed to his head and said, 'It is here.'

Insanity was an obvious defence and was supported by two doctors, who argued that Jesse was not responsible for his actions. They blamed a form of epilepsy and agreed when the prosecution put forward the point that Jesse showed no remorse and didn't seem able to realise what horrific suffering he'd caused. The jury found for the prosecution and recommended that Jesse be imprisoned rather than suffer the death penalty. The judge ignored their counsel and sentenced him to hang.

Although there were those who were baying for his blood, Jesse also had supporters who thought that such a young boy could not possibly have known the enormity of his actions. Petitions were drawn up, both for and against commuting his sentence. His case attracted attention in high places, but nonetheless mercy was denied him. The warrant for his execution was sent to the governor of the state for his authorisation. Once this was signed, Jesse Pomeroy would become the second child under the age of sixteen to be hanged in Massachusetts.

The controversy raged on. A newspaper published what was said to be Jesse's autobiography. In it (again, there must be a suspicion that he was not the actual author), he insisted on his innocence. Referring to the boys who had identified him as the perpetrator of the first series of attacks he wrote: 'Not one of them did or could tell what dress I wore or how my voice sounded – in fact, they failed to notice everything a sharp boy would and fell back on the untenable ground of identifying me by my eye.'

His first confession, he claimed, was the result of police harassment. They had awoken him in the middle of the night and forced it out of him with threats. The subsequent trial was a sham: 'The complaints were read to me and I understood them about as much as I would

Greek or Latin.' The result was 'Not justice dealt out, but rather injustice.' He took the same line in respect of the two murders, saying that he'd not been anywhere near the marshes where Horace Mullen had been discovered, and had made a full account of his whereabouts on the day of the killing. His confession on this occasion had been an attempt to protect his mother and his brother, who had been wrongly imprisoned for a number of weeks. 'The jury,' he said, were 'twelve jackasses, good and true.'

Mrs Pomeroy, faced with conclusive evidence to the contrary, continued to live in denial. When she read that her son had confessed in order to help her she said, 'I was not surprised – I knew Jesse better than anyone and I knew his generous heart.' She wrote to newspapers and set up a one-woman campaign to prove her son's innocence. The death sentence was a great injustice, she insisted, and Jesse had to be saved at all costs. Her voice, combined with that of such people as the famous writer Oliver Wendell Holmes, had its effect and the governor prevaricated over Jesse's fate. It may have been the case that he didn't want the death of a fifteen-year-old boy on his conscience, of course, but he must equally have felt the need to appease those voters who demanded vengeance. Finally, he was able to 'pass the buck' to his successor, who also baulked at the final signature. Two years later, the state's Executive Council, who had always pressed for Jesse's death, relented. They commuted the sentence to life imprisonment but – and here their motives are suspect – Jesse was to spend his entire sentence in solitary confinement.

For sixteen years, Jesse Pomeroy saw only the walls of an eight-foot square cell. He had no visitors apart from his mother (whom he was allowed to see once every month). His only other human contact was with prison officers and the chaplain. In the early years of the new century, he was transferred to a more modern cell but his solitary confinement was to continue for 41 years.

His overall preoccupation was escape. He spent much of his time planning various unsuccessful attempts, which were reported in the newspapers – thereby keeping his name before an ever-interested public. His best endeavour was in 1888, when he managed to dig a small hole in his cell wall through which, by means of a broken piece of piping, he was able to permeate the gap between his wall and the next one with gas. His ruse was unsuccessful: when he put a light to the gas, there was an enormous bang and Jesse was left with singed eyebrows and some minor damage to prison property to account for.

He immersed himself in books. He read all the eight thousand volumes available in the prison library and managed in the process to teach himself French, German, Greek, Latin, Spanish and Italian, as well as learning the intricacies of the American legal code. Without any hope of eventual freedom he might well have gone insane, but he hung onto a forlorn chance of winning a pardon through the legal process. Freeing such a high-profile prisoner would never prove to be a vote winner and he was turned down by all twelve of the state governors he appealed to. Thirty-eight years into his sentence, three psychiatrists and the prison doctor submitted a report on Jesse's mental health and the possibility of his punishment having finally taught him the error of his ways. The effects of a lifetime's solitary confinement does seem to have been taken into account in their summary for, though they said Jesse was sane and intelligent, they also referred to him as a cold, paranoid manipulator, utterly obsessed with the matter of his pardon. Their report stated:

> *He takes kindness as a matter of course, is highly egotistical and inclined to dictate to the prison authorities. His only interest in his mother is the aid she can give him in securing his release. He shows no pleasure at seeing her but begins on his case as soon as she comes and talks of nothing else. He is very unreliable on account of his untruthfulness. He thinks everyone is against him and apparently never loses his suspicions for a moment.*

None of this is at all surprising, especially the issue of freedom, given the circumstances. Unfortunately for Jesse, his mother, who despite his apparent indifference must have been a welcome monthly visitor, died soon after their comments were written. The panel of doctors were bemused to learn that Jesse strongly supported the idea of harsh punishment. He didn't go as far as to think this should apply to himself, though. As a report stated: 'His memory is very good except on points the admission of which might weaken his case.'

It was to be another two years before he was allowed out of solitary confinement. Again, one can detect a note of vague surprise in the written assessments of his character, which seem to take no account of his treatment. The Commissioner of Corrections, A Warren Stearns, wrote: 'He engaged in no occupation, never participated in prison industries and was seen as a gradually aging old man, nearly blind, with a tremendous hernia, standing about impassive and solitary, not taking part in any of the social life of the institution.'

By 1920 Jesse had the dubious honour of being America's best-known prisoner. He appeared in public for the first time since his trial and performed in the prison's annual minstrel show where he read one of his poems to an enthusiastic audience of inmates and warders. In 1921 he published his writings in a book entitled *Selections from the Writings of Jesse Harding Pomeroy*. The contents were a mixed bag of jottings such as 'How I Learned Spanish', 'A Boston Brew of Tea, Sir!' and 'A La Miss Suffragette'. It was reviewed as a book of 'no intrinsic merit'.

Jesse outlived all the people who had sat in judgement over him: the judge, the council and the twelve jurors. There were always people on the outside who vocalised their belief that this protracted imprisonment was a scandal. In the late 20s, when he had become the oldest prisoner in the state, he successfully sued a woman for libel. She had written to a newspaper confirming the widely-spread rumour that Jesse had been cruel to animals whilst in prison. He won the case and was awarded the derisory amount of one dollar in damages. Presumably he didn't find out about the existence of Guy Logan's book *Rope, Knife and Chair*, which portrayed him as the killer of 27 boys and girls, some of whom had been nailed to doors.

Much against his will, he was transferred to the State Prison Farm in 1929. This was to be his first experience of the outside world in 53 years. He was driven there in an automobile and, as John Marr puts it: 'Virtually every two-bit pen jockey in the country seized the opportunity to comment on how strange the outside world must seem to this modern Rip van Winkle after 53 years "inside". Poor Jesse unwittingly found himself the springboard for countless bad metaphors and half-baked musing on fifty years of progress.'

The transfer was not a happy one. Jesse was, by now, incapable of handling even the small amount of freedom the law now allowed him. He was 'dissatisfied, peevish, almost surly'. He was blind in one eye and losing his sight in the other, and had a massive hernia. He was no longer a celebrated prisoner, able to sell his photograph for $1.50 a time. He was a decrepit old man who, despite everything, made another pathetic attempt to escape.

He died on 29 September 1932, just short of his 73rd birthday. He had spent 53 years in jail.

PETER AND JOHN

In Britain, in 1861, the *Chester Chronicle* reported the trial of Peter Henry Barratt and John Bradley, both only eight years of age. They were indicted on a charge of the wilful murder of George Burgess, in the northern town of Stockport, England.

George was the son of Richard Burgess, a weaver who lived at Higher Hillgate, in the town. The little boy was two years and three months old. His father had seen him at ten minutes to two on 9 April, playing about ten yards from the door of the house where he (George) lived with a nursemaid, Sarah Ann Warren. No mention is made of George's mother, who had, presumably, either died or left her home at some earlier date.

George was with one of his friends, Samuel Burton. Seeing that all seemed to be in order, Burgess went off to work. When he returned that evening just before seven o'clock, he was told that George was missing. He immediately went to Sarah Warren's house and joined in the search for his son.

George's nurse Sarah lived in nearby Shaw Cross Street. She had seen George alive and well at quarter past two; at that time he was playing on waste ground in front of the house. Half an hour later he had disappeared. She spent the rest of the day – and much of the night – looking for him. In the early hours of the morning, the pair reluctantly abandoned their search until the next day.

The *Chester Chronicle* reported witnesses who later saw George in the company of two older boys. Almost two hundred years later, the Bulger case was to show chilling similarities to this one: two children leading a toddler away; a brutal attack; and adult witnesses who saw nothing amiss at the time, but whose accounts, when pieced together, form a record of the last few hours of a toddler's life.

A Mary Whitehead reported that on Thursday afternoon, 11 April, she had seen the little boy being led along by the other two. They were near her house in Love Lane and were walking rather quickly. The larger of the older boys had George by the hand and he was crying. She noted that the toddler was properly dressed except for the fact that he wasn't wearing his cap. She asked them where they were going and, maybe facetiously, they gave her the self-evident answer that they were going down Love Lane. The youngest child did not seem to be going very willingly. At this point Mrs Whitehead wasn't sure if the child was a boy or a girl. One of his companions said he was a boy.

Love Lane, where Mrs Whitehead lived, ran alongside Ford's Fields. This, it transpired, was where the children were headed. Another witness, young Frank Williams, said he was in the garden with his mother that afternoon when he saw the three boys. He also told of how the small child was being led by the hand, but said that at the point when he saw him, George was naked. One of the older boys took a twig out of a nearby hedge and hit George. The only provocation appeared to have been that George had stopped to rub his leg.

Emma Williams (presumably Frank's mother, though this is not stated) said she saw the group in the field itself. She confirmed what Frank had said: that the youngest child was naked. Emma called out to the three:

[I] asked them what they were doing with the child undressed. They did not make any answer. I called again and they went in the direction of the brook. The first time I called they were going up the field, and when I called a second time they went down in the direction of the brook, which was going farther from me. When they turned they went down by the hedge in the direction of the trees. I could not see for the trees which way the children went.[2]

George's body was found on the following day by a John Butler. There was a brook running through Ford's Fields and Butler was working nearby. At about noon, he saw something that looked like a child lying face-down in the water. Closer investigation revealed that it was a small boy, naked except for his clogs and with the water only just covering his head. He realised at once that nothing could be done for the child and sent for the police.

Inspector William Walker of Stockport police arrived quickly. He said:

I received information about half past twelve o'clock that the body of a child was in the brook. I found the body of a child there lying on its face. When I took it out of the water its nose was flat and turned on one side, as if the head had been pressed downwards, and underneath the nose I found a large stone. The body was naked with the exception of the clogs. I observed marks on the body as if he had been struck with a stick. I found the clothes about eight yards from the body. The clothes were higher up, further from the bridge. They were in the brook with the exception of one stocking which was on the land, about ten yards from the body and about twenty from where I found the clothes. The stocking was nearer the bridge than the body, and was quite dry. The banks were not steep; if the child had fallen in it could have got out again. There were footmarks where the body and clothes were found. They were large where the clothes were found. I sent a man with the body to the White Horse tavern and followed it. That was the same body examined by Mr Massey, the surgeon, and it was in the same condition.[3]

Thomas Massey made the post-mortem examination on 13 April. He confirmed that these were the remains of a strong and healthy child. On parts of the torso and legs Massey discovered a number of light scratches and bruises that appeared to have been caused by a blunt instrument or stick. The lower part of the body was covered with bruises, which had a striped appearance. The flesh beneath the skin was, as he put it: 'much infiltrated with blood, which was a sign of the violence having been severe'. He went on:

I did not notice anything on the exterior of the head. I removed the scalp and on the right side there was a large scratch – the size of a five-shilling piece – between the scalp and the skull, which would require great violence to produce it. Such a blow upon a live child would probably have stunned it. I saw a small patch on the left side of the forehead. I think it possible that a stick that produced the other bruises would have produced these two on the scalp. I found the lungs congested; the great vessels at the root of the heart and lungs were gorged with black blood; the liver was also congested. I believe the cause of death was suffocation or drowning. The marks were produced while the child was alive.[4]

When he was cross-examined in court, Massey confirmed that the injuries on the head were internal. Sometimes, he told the jury, a blow on one side of the brain produces an effect on the other side. A child will bleed more easily than a grown-up person. He couldn't tell whether the injuries beneath the scalp were occasioned before or after death: in his opinion, though, death had been caused by drowning. The scratches might have been produced by a naked child going through a hedge. The injury on the forehead might have been produced by a fall.

Another member of the jury put forward the supposition that George might have fallen down the sides of the brook and, as he entered the water, hit his head on a stone. Massey disagreed: 'It* must have been dropped into the water perpendicularly with its head downwards, and its head must have struck against a sharp stone to produce such an effect. The vessels of the brain were congested, which was [a] symptom of death by drowning.'

---

* In the report of this case, many of the witnesses and the two accused refer to George as 'it' rather than 'he'. Presumably this pronoun stands for 'the baby' and was a convention of the time.

In a relatively small town such as Stockport (especially in that period) neighbours would soon be able to identify two local boys. It seems that Peter Barratt and John Bradley had, in any case, made no attempt to hide who they were. On 13 April a police officer, William Morley, called at Peter Barratt's house. The following conversation took place with the boy's father present and, it seems, John Bradley also in the room:*

'Do you go to school?' Morley began.

'Yes, sometimes on a Sunday.'

'Who did you play with last Thursday afternoon?'

Barratt replied that he'd been with 'Jemmy' Bradley and they had been 'aside of Star Inn'. This was true enough: Star Inn was relatively near Love Lane and Ford's Field but Barratt was avoiding the main point of the question. Morley pressed him gently: 'Where did you go then?'

Barratt was not about to lie but, though each of his answers is truthful to a degree, none elaborate more than is required by the particular question. 'Down a narrow lane by the Star Inn,' he said. 'Down Henshull Lane and up Love Lane.'

Morley asked Barratt if he'd seen anybody in Love Lane. Barratt's friend, Bradley, answered for him. The report states that he seemed anxious to say something.

'Only a woman,' he replied. Asked if she had had anything to say to them, Bradley told the officer that she'd asked them where they were going. At this point, no mention had been made of George. Morley, who appears to have been very considerate to the young

---

* Bradley is introduced into the report without preamble. Either he was with the Barratts when Morley called or the newspaper has cobbled two different interviews together. The former explanation is the more likely.

suspects, now asked them if there was anyone else with them. It appears that neither of the boys had any idea at all of the gravity of the situation. Bradley's answer is truthful, but (maybe artfully) nonchalant: 'Only a little lad we met by the Star Inn.'

Now addressing himself to Bradley alone, Morley asked where they went after Love Lane. Bradley told him: 'We went down Love Lane, and we came to a hole with some water in it.' He had to be prompted yet again but, when Morley asked him, he went on: 'Peter said we must undress him.'

Here Barratt interrupted. The tale was approaching what he knew to be the crucial point and he wasn't about to accept sole responsibility for what had happened: 'Well, thou undressed him as well as me,' he said indignantly.

Morley clarified the matter by saying: 'Then you both undressed him?' to which they both answered 'Yes'. Morley went on: 'What did you do with him then?'

Bradley said, 'Peter pushed it in the water. I took my clogs off, went in and took it out. And Peter said it must have another.'

'Another what?'

Bradley replied, 'Another dip in the water. Peter got a stick out of the hedge and hit it.'

Barratt jumped in again: 'Well, thou hit it as well as me.'

'Then you both hit it?' Morley asked. Both boys replied, 'Yes'.

Morley asked them how often they beat 'it' with the stick. The youngsters made no attempt to claim George's death was accidental. 'Till it was dead,' Bradley said.

'Was it in the water?' Morley asked. He later said that he couldn't be certain that both agreed to this but he thought so. He was sure that neither boy contested the fact: 'one said it and the other heard it'. He went on to check the details of the assault on George, no doubt to make sure that the boys weren't merely seeking infamy for some fanciful reasons.

'Where did you beat it?'

'Over the back.'

'Did you hit it anywhere else besides over the back?'

'Yes, over the head, but not much.'

'Did you leave it in the water when you came away?'

'Yes.'

Both boys were taken to the police cells. Details were checked: they had claimed to have thrown the stick they had used for beating George into a field, so it was useless to search for it. However, on 14 April, Morley took Barratt's shoes and Bradley's clogs to the brook and was able to confirm that the prints left there corresponded exactly with the boys' footwear.

Despite their direct and apparently unemotional answers to his questions, Morley said both boys seemed agitated. His evidence, along with that of the inspector, the surgeon and the witnesses who'd seen George being led away to his death, made up the case for the Prosecution. The Defence was left with the difficult task of either making a case for the boys' total innocence (not very promising, especially in the light of their admissions), or appealing to the jury's charity by stressing the boys' youth.

Mr Morgan Lloyd tried a hotchpotch of these two tactics. To begin with he 'dwelt at some length on the tender years of the prisoners and suggested the improbability of their having committed the grave offence with which they stood charged. [The] deceased might have been bathing and got drowned, or he might have fallen down in the water when attempting to cross the bridge over the brook.'[5]

Mr Lloyd hoped the jury would place no reliance upon the statement made by Morley about the confessions the boys had made. He put forward that 'there was nothing easier than for a police officer – or a barrister for that matter – to get any answer he pleased by putting leading questions.'

Knowing his argument to be extremely weak, Mr Lloyd covered his options by telling the jury that if they were of the opinion that the deceased *had* met with his death at the hands of the prisoners, then it must have been as a result of childish play. They could not have known the nature of the crime they were committing; it must have happened during a 'bout of boyish mischief' since the accused were unable to know right from wrong. Mr Lloyd made what the newspaper described as a powerful appeal (it appears more to have been a rather desperate one) '. . . and sat down', the report stated, 'fully relying on the jury acquitting the prisoners.'

The jury retired to consider the verdict at ten o'clock. After an absence of a quarter of an hour they returned into court with a verdict of 'Manslaughter'. The judge told them that he quite agreed. The prisoners would be sent to a reformatory, where they would be taken care of.

The *Chester Chronicle* gave a report of his speech:

. . . They would thus be removed from their bad companions at Stockport; they would be taught better things and have a chance of becoming better boys. If they behaved themselves properly there, the government might dismiss them before the full period of the sentence had expired.

Prisoners at the bar, I am afraid you have been very wicked, naughty boys, and I have no doubt you have caused the death of this little boy by the brutal way in which you used him. I am going to send you to a place where you will have an opportunity of becoming good boys, for there you will have a chance of being brought up in a way you should be, and I doubt not but that in time when you come to understand the nature of the crime you have committed, you will repent of what you have done. The sentence is that each of you be imprisoned and kept in gaol for one month, and at the expiration of that period you are to be sent to a reformatory for five years.

The paper concluded its report by saying:

The little fellows received the sentence with a sort of laugh and cry mixture on their faces, one looking at the other, evidently wondering what the scene or sentence could mean. Bradley shed a few tears when Mr M Lloyd was addressing the jury, but they were soon dried up, giving place to a laugh which the little fellow indulged in, his eye having caught something which tickled his fancy. Barratt on the whole was more serious than his companion, although he smiled now and then.

The persons in Court testified their approval of the verdict and sentence by loud acclamations which could not be suppressed before several minutes had elapsed.

3. THE BOY WHO LOVED POISONS

Graham Young loved his Aunt Win and Uncle Jack. He loved them so much he neglected to poison them.

Everyone else he came into contact with – friends, family, workmates – was at risk. As long as they drank tea and ate sandwiches, no matter what they were to him, they suited Graham's purpose. Tea and sandwiches were part of Graham's stock-in-trade, but almost anything would serve: a glass of wine; water, even. Graham knew which poisons tasted and which didn't; he knew exactly which doses would kill and which would merely send his 'subject' into agonies. He didn't poison out of hatred, or greed. He did it because he was interested in poisons and their effects. He was motivated by a scientist's single-minded preoccupation. This studious boy saw the world as one big laboratory and himself as the dispassionate vivisector. 'I don't see them as human beings,' he said of his victims once. 'I see them as guinea pigs.'

Some boys might have dreams of becoming a soldier, a footballer, or an astronaut; Graham scorned such petty aspirations. He knew his talents were special and he was determined to hone them, to develop them and to use them to the very best effect. His life was going to be a much greater adventure than his friends would find depicted by their ridiculous comic-book heroes: Graham Young's ambition was to have an effigy of himself standing in the Chamber of Horrors at Madame

Tussaud's waxworks alongside the murderers Dr Crippen and John Reginald Christie. He wanted the world to remember him as one of its most prolific killers.

Despite the undoubted pain and horrible suffering he caused, Young's geekish personality, and the fact that he was only fourteen years old when he began his macabre 'experiments', make him the sort of killer history doesn't take quite seriously. His youthful enthusiasm and his detailed knowledge of every aspect of his 'hobby' might just as easily have been directed towards stamp collecting or model aeroplanes – even chemistry *per se* – but no: he was interested in poison and that was that. His stepmother (in particular) tried to stop him. She even forbad him to bring toxic substances into the house, but he dodged her with ease and continued to dabble with his beloved little phials and bottles in spite of her objections. She then became, so far as Young was concerned, as good a subject for his experiments as anyone else: he carefully noted the effects of each dose he gave her and was delighted with his first real success when, in 1962, she died. Her long, debilitating illness had no discernable cause; she herself had put it down to a traffic accident when she'd hit her head on the roof of the bus in which she had been travelling. Graham persuaded his father to have her cremated – he said it was the modern way and he rather insisted upon it. Once the ashes had been scattered, nobody would dream of suspecting that Mrs Young's death was suspicious. Even if they did, who could prove anything against her bookish stepson?

Graham was never charged with his stepmother's death. He had committed the perfect murder. If he had stopped there, nobody would ever have known that he'd done it. Unfortunately, he carried on. Maybe there was a part of him that wanted the public to know how clever he'd been; maybe he was revelling in his grisly achievement; or maybe he simply couldn't help himself. Whatever his reasons, he had started to administer doses of antimony and belladonna to his family. In his stepmother's case, he'd been very clever indeed: he'd used thallium. This virulent substance is virtually undetectable and, outside a certain Agatha Christie novel,* no one in Britain had ever been accused of using it for the purpose of murder. It has no colour or flavour; it has been much used in Iraq for the disposal of inconvenient people who are no longer useful to the security forces.

Graham Frederick Young was born in 1947, two years after the end of Second World War, in Neasden, a dull, respectable suburb of north-west London. Psychiatrists could now, no doubt, discern from the first few months of his life some of the reasons for the extraordinary teenager and the adult he was to become. At the time of his birth, his mother developed pleurisy and therefore wasn't able to give him the physical security we now believe to be so important. Her illness worsened and she became a victim of tuberculosis. She died just before Christmas, only a couple of months after Graham's arrival. Graham's father, Fred, was left with a new baby and an eight-year-old daughter, Winifred. As so often happened in those days, the extended family rallied round. Winifred went to live with her grandmother. Win, Fred's sister, and her husband, Jack, agreed to look after the baby. They already had one child, Sandra, but once Graham came into their lives, Win and Jack regarded him as their own

---

* *The Pale Horse.*

son. It seemed as though he was going to be all right after all.

He was a sickly child, but he liked his cousin and loved his 'Aunty Panty' and 'Daddy Jack'. He did display some peculiarities: even at the tender age of eighteen months, he would scribble over the walls of his bedroom with pencils he'd managed to purloin from Jack's pocket. More worryingly, he would rock violently backwards and forwards. He would even do this in his sleep, and sometimes it was so forceful that it prompted the man next door to complain about the thumping. This sure sign of distress was a problem nobody knew, how to deal with. In the end, it was accepted as something the family would just have to put up with. Graham's rocking was an idiosyncrasy, and there was nothing they could do about it. They called it the 'dig-digs'. Today this behaviour would be investigated. Back in the late 40s, it was shrugged at.

Fred didn't neglect his family. He would take Winifred to see her baby brother every week and they would go for walks around the district. He wanted very much for them all to be together again, but in those days the idea of a man running a household was simply not entertained. Fred began to think about the possibility of marrying again.

He met Molly, who became his wife in 1950 and was to become Graham's first victim. After the wedding, Graham was taken away from his beloved Aunty Panty and Daddy Jack and brought back to live with his immediate family. It didn't seem to be a problem. He was able to see his aunt and uncle very frequently and he appeared to be devoted to Molly, following her around the house. She, in her turn, loved him enormously. Fred must have felt relieved that at long last his life was back together again.

Graham grew into a chubby, freckled boy whose nickname was 'Pudding'. He wasn't keen on sports and didn't seem to mix with other children, but nor did he appear to be in the least bit unhappy. His sister, with hindsight, recalled that there may have been signs but, no doubt, the family were so thankful to see things working out that they wouldn't want to read anything into the little boy's innocent quirks. She said that he never developed any hobbies of any sort and always preferred the company of older people to those of children his own age. As a child he liked to sit on park benches and chat to old men rather than mix with other young children.

It may have had something to do with his intelligence; he was always extremely bright and did very well at school. His aptitude in maths may have left something to be desired but his English and history were both very good indeed, and he was an avid reader. In many ways he conformed to the stereotype of the schoolboy 'swot'. What his family didn't know was that all those hours in the local library were spent in slowly acquiring a prodigious knowledge of toxic substances.

His grandmother later recalled that, from the age of nine, small bottles fascinated him. He would take any that had a distinctive odour: nail varnish, perfume, smelling salts and the like. His stepmother once found acid burns on his school blazer. She quizzed him about this, and he finally admitted that he'd been searching through the dustbins of a nearby chemist's shop.

He liked to be able to show off. He would produce bottles from his pocket and ask people to smell them. When they had done that, he would reel off the different components that had gone to make the aroma. Though he was often laconic he would suddenly volunteer reams of information: these always involved items that seemed strange coming from the mouth of a child. There was the occasion, for instance, when he told Sandra that an aspirin could burn the lining of the stomach if taken without food. His sister said he had a habit of taking a contrary point of view – not, she maintained, in an aggressive way, but simply playing devil's advocate in order to keep the discussion alive.

He was neat and tidy and wasn't, as other disturbed children have been, cruel. It seems he loved animals, and would go around with his pet budgie perched on his finger.

He did have other hobbies apart from chemistry. At a very early age he became fascinated with Adolf Hitler. He had a swastika badge and had also drawn the symbol on an armband that he loved to wear. It wasn't the most popular of interests – especially at that time when the memories of the sacrifices and horrors of war were still fresh in everybody's mind – but, as wise parents knew, then as now, the best thing was to let such obsessions die a natural death. He was very keen on black magic, and had expressed a desire to join a coven. He liked Dracula, too, and his big hero was the Victorian poisoner Dr William Palmer. None of this morbidity is particularly unusual for teenage boys. As the local librarian said when Molly asked him to keep a check on Graham's reading material, boys are bound to be interested in vile subjects that would horrify their mums and dads. Graham, he was sure, would grow out of it in time.

But Graham didn't grow out of it. He was something of an embarrassment to his cousin, Sandra, who didn't take too kindly to his more provocative acts such as ostentatiously smoking on a bus immediately after insisting that he should only pay half fare; knocking drinks out of the hands of a waitress; kicking someone's suitcase at the tube station, or embarrassing a woman in a waiting room by staring her out. Nowadays, these tiny acts of rebellion would be regarded as not untypical, but this was a period when children wouldn't normally have dared to misbehave so openly. Sandra once pointed out a friend of hers to him: 'That's Jacqueline's boyfriend, Jim,' she said. Graham (perhaps getting 'hooked' on the alliteration) repeated the phrase over and over, putting it in the form of a question and then answering himself: 'Is that Jacqueline's boyfriend Jim?' 'I think it's Jacqueline's boyfriend Jim.' In this, in his obsessions, in his amazingly retentive memory for technical terms, in his solitary nature and in his infant habit of rocking backwards and forwards, he was showing some of the symptoms of autism. It seems he was never diagnosed with such a condition.

In 1961 Winifred met Denis, whom she was later to marry. She thinks it is possibly because of her having meals at Denis's house that she managed to avoid the illnesses that beset the rest of her family, although she wasn't completely to escape. One day she was on her way to meet Denis at a cinema in nearby Willesden, when she was violently sick outside the underground station. It had been about an hour since she had drunk a cup of tea Graham had given her. It wasn't the first time she had felt like this and it wouldn't be the last: on each occasion she was poisoned, her face drained of all colour, and she became terribly ill until there was nothing left in her stomach and she brought up bile. The effects would wear off quite quickly and it was to be some years before she found out what had caused them.

Like the good scientist he was, Graham didn't murder as a matter of course: there were times when he would feel it equally beneficial to let the person live and to observe the effects of smaller doses of poison. Perhaps by mistake, perhaps as part of his research, he also managed to poison himself – but, of course, he was able to cure himself just as easily.

It might seem incredible that a whole family could suffer from stomach cramps, vomiting, hallucinations and dizziness and not suspect the intense little boy whose greatest passion was how to cause just such effects. But they rationalised the symptoms in other ways: 'It was something in the water supply'; 'It was a bug that was going around' – Molly, Graham's step-mother, assumed that her terrible symptoms were the after-effects of the road accident she had been involved in; the doctors thought she had an ulcer. If, at any time, Graham was thought responsible, it was believed he'd carelessly used one of their cups for his noxious substances. 'Careless' was certainly not the appropriate word here. Graham Young later described his methods:

> I started experimenting at home, putting sometimes one, and sometimes three, grains on prepared foods which my mother, father and sister ate. By September of last year [it was 1962 when he wrote this] it became an obsession with me, and I continued giving members of my family antimony tartrate on prepared foods. My mother lost weight all the time through it, and I stopped giving it to her about February this year. After my mother died on 21 April 1962, I started putting antimony tartrate in milk and water my father was drinking. As a result he became critically ill and was taken to hospital. I knew the doses I was giving were

not fatal, but I knew I was doing wrong. It grew on me like a drug habit, except that it was not me who was taking the drug.[1]

One day his sister was sent home from work. She had begun to feel ill on the way there: the world swam before her eyes, and she lost control over her movements. Things seemed to become larger, and then smaller. Her boss sent her to Middlesex Hospital, where tests revealed that she was suffering from the effects of belladonna poisoning. She immediately thought of Graham and his 'little friends' – the bottles he'd been forbidden to have in the house. Of course, she thought, he must have been playing around secretly and this was the result. He deserved to be severely reprimanded and shown that he really must stop this dangerous hobby. Surely when he realised what he had done he would be contrite.

Not a bit of it. Graham was indignant and very upset when confronted. He began to cry, and stomped off to his room. He told his sister she was wicked to have suspected him. The belladonna could just as easily have come from shampoo – Winifred might not be aware that shampoos contained it but he, Graham, knew this and plenty of other things about it. He was vehement, and Winifred felt terrible that the thought had ever entered her head. Her apology was accepted.

Graham wasn't going to stop just because he'd had such a close shave. He carried on buying his chemicals and poisons from chemist shops. He always signed the poison register ME Evans and claimed he needed the substances for a science teacher at school. Some chemists were suspicious but he was able to persuade them as soon as he started displaying his detailed scientific knowledge. He also, naturally, convinced them that he was older than he actually was.

Having disposed of his stepmother, Graham turned his attention to his father. Winifred, worried about Fred's sudden inability to take food, suggested that he take the invalid drink, Benger's Food, as it would at least put something in his stomach. Graham was quite happy to administer this – along with increasing doses of antimony. Fred, unsurprisingly, didn't seem to respond to any treatment. His illness grew worse and he lost weight but he was, as he always had been, reluctant to see a doctor. His family realised that he was feeling especially awful when, at last, he gave in to their entreaties and went along to the family doctor without putting up his usual resistance. He was referred to a hospital for tests, but these were unable to reveal the basis of his trouble. Graham, of course, had known all along they wouldn't be able to: antimony is virtually undetectable unless you know what you're looking for.

It shows something for Winifred (and her aunt's) persistence that after a second visit and a second referral, the hospital – absolutely aghast at their own findings – declared that Fred Young was suffering from poisoning: 'It was either arsenic or antimony'. They came to the reasonable conclusion that he had administered the stuff himself, possibly out of grief following Molly's death. But Graham's aunt and his sister had other ideas.

Fred was lucky. Had he taken just one more dose of antimony, he would almost certainly have perished. Graham, who didn't really need a rational motive for his crimes, later confessed that he had administered doses of antimony every time his father had told him off. He had not only chosen that particular poison because its effects were difficult to diagnose, but had also decided it wouldn't be a good idea for his father to suffer the same symptoms as his stepmother. Therefore it was thallium for one, antimony for the other. The only link between the two – not lost on his family – was that the studious little boy, whom they were now seeing in a different light, knew all about them both.

He didn't try to hide his knowledge, either. He felt superior to the doctors who couldn't tell the difference between antimony and arsenic and said so over and over.

Aunt Win and sister Winfred knew for certain Graham was behind all this but tried desperately to push the thought out of their heads: it was simply too awful to contemplate. Aunt Win went as far as to put to him: 'Are you doing anything? I don't want you to be silly about this, so tell me if you're doing anything.' He replied that he wasn't and his face betrayed not one jot of dishonesty. Aunt Win, despite herself, breathed a sigh of relief, but Graham's assurance did not take away that niggling doubt at the back of her mind. She recalled how Graham had watched his father writhing in agony and had accurately predicted every stage of his decline. Fred himself had seen something in his son's behaviour and had recognised it for what it was. He had at one point said that he didn't want Graham to visit him in hospital. It was worrying. Very worrying indeed.

Aunt Win was now wise enough to make sure Graham was never alone with any food or drink. She tried to tell herself that, if he was responsible, it was some appalling mistake that he didn't want to admit to. He might have continued to get away with several more killings. The fact that a fourteen-year-old boy could poison his family was so incredible as not to be believed.

Luckily his poisoning career was brought to a temporary halt: his science teacher had become suspicious.

Graham was something of a loner but he did have one friend at school. His name was Christopher Williams. A petty squabble between them ended up with Chris getting the better of Graham and Graham saying that he would kill Chris. Chris forgot about the disagreement, and didn't recall what Graham had said when he (Chris) started having acute bilious attacks, painful, debilitating headaches and cramps in his arms and legs. Not one to hide his macabre hobby even at the risk of incriminating himself, Graham had been bringing various substances to school to do tests in the chemistry lab. His teacher, slightly concerned by this, had gone through Graham's desk and had found an exercise book which contained notes, drawings and even poems, all on the subject of poison and poisoners. Thinking all this extremely unhealthy, and with Chris's mysterious illness nagging at his memory, the teacher contacted the headmaster, who in turn contacted the Young's family doctor. When they were told of Fred's similarly unexplained symptoms, they knew they had to do something about it. Their first action was to book Graham in to see the school psychiatrist: he would find out if there was anything in the boy's character unusual enough to warrant their taking things further.

If there was one flaw in Graham's strategies, it was his inability to hide his unhealthy passions, particularly when there was any chance to show off his knowledge in front of someone who flattered him. The psychiatrist only had to butter him up very slightly and Graham's obsession came spilling out. An objective person had at last made the connection between the boy with the passion for poison and the various illnesses that seemed to follow in his wake. The police were informed, and Graham was arrested.

Graham's supply of little bottles was discovered: not only the ones he was carrying with him when he arrived home from school that day in May 1962, but also the amazing array he had in his bedroom, those he had hidden in a hedge, and a further cache stored away in a hut at a nearby reservoir.

Graham didn't appear to be overly concerned at his arrest. Some time ago Winifred, fed up with his hero worship of the murderer Dr William Palmer, had said to him that Palmer couldn't have been all that clever as he'd ended up on the gallows. Graham had simply said that they wouldn't hang him nowadays because there wasn't any capital punishment. No, Winifred had retorted, they would send him to prison for the rest of his life. Graham had shrugged and said, 'Oh, well. That's nothing.'

Prior to his trial, he was sent to a juvenile remand centre where, despite his general demeanour, he tried to hang himself. This may have been a grand gesture which was never actually intended to work; it may have followed a sudden realisation of what he had actually done; or it may have been, as he told a psychiatrist, that he was missing the feeling of power he achieved from having his poisons around him.

In the dock, in the daunting surroundings of the Old Bailey, Graham Young was quite relaxed and at home. He sat there in his school blazer and grey flannels, a smaller than average boy with his legs crossed, displaying no signs of remorse or fear. He pleaded guilty to the charges against him: there were three in all. His stepmother's murder was not part of the indictment: Graham's suggestion that she be cremated had disposed of the evidence.

Psychiatrists testifying for the prosecution concluded that Graham Young was a dangerous psychopath and was more than likely to repeat his experiments if given half a chance. He was sentenced to fifteen years detention in Broadmoor, a top security hospital for the criminally insane. He was the second youngest patient to be sent there.

Incredibly, his family, with one important exception, felt sorry for him and stayed by him. Winifred saw him as little more than a child who was 'sick, terribly, dreadfully sick'. She tried to reason her way through the fog of disbelief and heartache: Graham's general lack of remorse, occasionally contradicted by incredibly genuine apologies, must indicate something seriously wrong, she thought. Though it seemed far-fetched to her, she thought the only reasonable explanation for this bizarre phenomenon was Graham's loss of his real mother at such an early age. She might have been correct but, whatever caused it, the illness would remain with Graham throughout his entire life, despite his attempts to disguise it.

Aunt Win, too, believed Graham was not responsible for his dreadful deeds. She always loved him as a son, and kept faith with her deep feelings throughout his life. His actions, never directed at her, nevertheless caused her terrible anguish but, to her, he was always the serious little boy she had taken in all that time ago, and she loved him despite everything. Only his father (not unreasonably) found it difficult to forgive the boy, especially for the death of Molly who, despite the lack of evidence, was certainly one of his victims.

Graham was heavily sedated when the three first went to see him. Naturally, he was well aware of what it was that the authorities had given him, and had tried to avoid having it administered. His appearance gave Winifred cause for disquiet. He was grey-skinned and greasy. He tapped his finger all the time and showed signs of agitation. Winifred couldn't remember what was said on that first visit except that it was emotional for all of them, including Graham.

Just about a month into his sentence a fellow inmate, one John Berridge, a 23-year-old ex-soldier, died in the middle of the night. It was found that he had somehow been poisoned with cyanide. Though officially his death was recorded as suicide, there were doubts. If Berridge had taken the cyanide himself, where had he acquired it? Maybe one of his visitors had sneaked it in; perhaps it had been sent to him through the post – then there were the laurel bushes in the grounds of the institution. These last might have been the most likely source had it not been for the fact that Berridge did not have the skills necessary to distil cyanide from laurel leaves. To do so would require considerable knowledge.

Graham Young was not formally charged over the death, though he (and it has to be said, many other patients) did claim it as his own doing. When asked why he'd done it, he explained that the man's snoring got on his nerves.

Graham was interested in his own condition, and in the medical histories of the other patients. Though the authorities tried to take his mind off chemicals and poisons, he was always able to tell patients exactly what was wrong with them. It was said that they never needed a doctor on Graham's ward. His own doctor confessed to swotting up on her knowledge of medicines prior to her visits because he knew so much about them and she didn't want to be caught out. He talked about his mental state lucidly enough. He made mention of hearing voices – it was his alter ego telling him to do things, he said. Eventually he would always bring the topic of conversation back to poisons, to Hitler or – his other favourite topic – his own trial, and how the public perceived the young poisoner.

He didn't like being confined and, as the years went on, he thought about ways of bringing his sentence to an end. There was only one way to get early release, of course, and that was to persuade his psychiatrists that he had been cured. This was going to be a long and difficult job for him: in order to be really convincing, he would have to keep off his favourite themes of conversation and become a model inmate. He was clever enough to do just that.

He would have to work hard at it. In a place full of odd people, Graham Young was seen as eccentric and isolated. He would stand for hours in the washrooms, looking at himself in the mirror, smiling and pulling faces. His interest in right-wing politics had continued unabated. He managed to obtain a copy of Hitler's manifesto *Mein Kampf*, and was thrilled when a retired social worker who had befriended him was 'good enough' to bring him back a present from her Austrian holiday: a brick from the Fuhrer's mountaintop 'Wolf's Lair' at Berchtesgaden. He supported Enoch Powell's radical views on racism and joined the far-right organisation the National Front, proudly wearing his NF tiepin. Later he made a brass swastika in the Broadmoor handicraft block. He wore it all the time and was seen kissing it whenever he thought nobody was watching him.

His tins for tea, sugar, powdered milk and the like were labelled: potassium cyanide, strychnine, vitriol, chloroform and sulphuric acid. He never watched TV or joined much in conversation. When people tried to talk to him he was scornful because they couldn't match his higher intelligence. He said to one of the nurses once that he 'only poisoned people whom he really liked'. He later added, 'I don't want to get to like you because I know you have a family.'

It seems incredible, but Graham was eventually given the job of making the tea for the staff. Maybe they thought themselves safe in an environment where it would be pretty impossible for the inmates to have any direct access to poisons. Resourceful as ever, however, Graham soon found a way of doctoring their drinks – with the lavatory cleaner, Harpic. They were fortunate, and didn't drink enough of the stuff to do themselves any serious damage. Graham confessed to what he had done and was punished with a stint of solitary confinement. He was taken off tea duty, of course, but later found another useful substance to pour into the kitchen tea urn: this time he used Manger's sugar soap. Again, they had a lucky escape when some fellow inmates discovered that the stuff was missing. One of them reported this incident, but it wasn't dealt with as it certainly should have been – and would have been, had it been anybody else who had made a deliberate attempt to poison the 97 men on that block. The inmates dealt out their own retribution and, naturally, scoured the urn thoroughly before they drank out of it again, but like his extremely dysfunctional behaviour and his strange enthusiasms, the file with the details of Graham's treachery was not to be held against him.

On 16 June 1970, just eight years after Graham was sentenced for administering poisons, Winifred received the following letter:

My dearest Win,

Many apologies from your wicked, neglectful brother, for failing to write to you for such an unconscionably long time. I really haven't had anything remotely interesting to write to you, and besides, when I think back on some of the mind-bending, utterly banal monologues which I've written to you in the past, I rather think that my omission may be counted a virtue rather than a sin!!

I have, however, some good news to import to you. I had an interview with the estimable Edgar [Dr Edgar Udwin, Graham's psychiatrist] last Friday, and he told me: 'Whether or not a formal recommendation has yet gone in, I have had several conversations with the Home Office about you, and I have got things moving at the end.' He also said, 'I am going to discharge you in the latter half of this year.'

As you see from my quotes, the pot is now almost boiling. Just think, Win, another few months and your friendly neighbourhood Frankenstein will be at liberty once again!!![2]

The 'estimable' Dr Udwin, who Graham had previously referred to as 'a fool' (as he did most people), was a South African and a senior psychiatrist at Broadmoor. He wrote his report in June 1970, saying that Graham's initial slow response to the treatment he had received was now resulting in 'profound changes'. Dr Udwin believed Graham was 'no longer obsessed with poisons, violence and mischief. And he was no longer a danger to others'.

Udwin had been disastrously wrong in his judgement once before. William Thomas Doyle had been sent to Broadmoor at the age of seventeen but was transferred to an ordinary hospital for the mentally ill three years later, prior to his release into the community. He had only been out eleven months when, using an iron bar, he murdered a hospital laundry worker. Dr Udwin had said of Doyle, 'I do not think he will be a danger to anyone at all. I regard him as no longer a security hazard.'

Perhaps a less obvious example of possible misjudgement was the case of Martin Victor Frape, who was sent to Parkhurst Jail (on the Isle of Wight) when Udwin said that the man was mentally fit to leave Broadmoor. He went on to lead a riot there, and held a prison officer at knife-point.

Graham Young's case, however, was regarded as unique. The Home Office decided that they had to take the views of his psychiatrist seriously, and Graham had successfully persuaded his keepers that he no longer felt the overwhelming impulse to experiment in poisons.

At Graham's first parole hearing, three years into his sentence, Aunt Win (despite her willingness to support him in the past) had agreed with his father that he was still dangerous. Fred Young went further: he later said that his son should never be released. Their opinions were only taken into account inasmuch as it was Winifred, rather than Fred, who was approached in October 1970. Her brother's release, she was told, would be in stages, beginning with a week's trial home leave. Would she and Denis be prepared to have him live with them and their baby? With Dr Udwin's assurances that Graham was now a safe person to have around, she agreed. She was brave enough and charitable enough to accept Udwin's opinion absolutely, telling herself that she would resist the urge to check on Graham during his week's leave. She wouldn't go running into the kitchen every time he was in there to make sure he wasn't doctoring their food or drink. If he was to have a chance of a normal life, as Winifred sincerely hoped he would, they had to put the past behind them and show him that they trusted in his cure.

Graham was good enough to leave Winifred and her family alone this time, though he was a difficult enough house guest anyway. Perhaps his personality might still have given an objective person plenty of cause for disquiet. He had a need to dominate the conversation, for instance. He couldn't bear it if somebody else in the room had an opinion; he had to be the sole authority and liked to lecture. His obsession with Hitler was tiresome and included forcing his hosts to listen to Wagner, Hitler's favourite composer. Winifred explained his oddities away, naturally enough, as the eccentricities of a boy who had been institutionalised since the age of fourteen, and who was bound to have severe problems adapting to life on the outside.

He went to Winifred again for his Christmas holiday that year. She was putting herself out considerably, not just because of whatever problems she may have had in persuading her husband to have her 'formerly' psychopathic brother in the house (she said Denis was happy about it) but also the practical considerations of squeezing three adults, a baby and a dog into their two bedrooms. She did tell him that once his permanent release arrived, it would be important for him to find his own place to live. He agreed, saying that he preferred to be independent.

It was a happy Christmas. Graham was very keen to show another side of himself and bought presents and cards for everyone, including a card for the dog. He even managed to behave reasonably well, if a little quietly, when they had friends around on Christmas Eve. When he got drunk on Christmas Day it was, again, seen as understandable in the light of his long incarceration. He apologised profusely the next day and appeared to be enjoying normal life, probably for the first time. Nevertheless, within four months, he would be buying poisons again.

Graham was 23 years old when he was released from custody. He was going to have severe problems adjusting but, with his superior intelligence and his desire to study, he would at least be able to earn a living. Whilst inside he had, somewhat audaciously, applied for membership of the Pharmaceutical Society and had also tried to get himself a job with a forensic laboratory. He was disappointed and genuinely surprised to be turned down for both on the grounds of his past history. He must have realised even then that the title of 'Britain's youngest poisoner' had its downside when it came to living in the real world and that it might be best to keep his achievements quiet, at least for the time being.

It is unlikely that his love of poisons ever really diminished, or even that there was a period around his release when he attempted to negate his macabre desires. The Home Secretary himself (at that time Reginald Maudling) was apparently dubious about Graham's supposed cure but supported the decisions of others in his department. Although Udwin's optimistic view prevailed, there were other psychiatrists on record with very different opinions. One, Dr Donald Blair, had examined the teenage Young at the time of his trial and had said there was no doubt in his mind that he was a very serious danger to other people. His intense obsession with drugs and their poisoning effects was not, he thought, likely to change. Graham Young could well repeat his cool, calm, calculating administration of the poisons at any time.

On Graham's former ward at Broadmoor, the senior nursing staff also had a file that noted his stated desire to murder one person for every year he had been locked away. It was not taken into account during the discussions about his release.

One of his fellow inmates at Broadmoor had no illusions. He saw Graham Young as a sadist with an evil personality that hid behind a gentle face. In him was an 'icy coldness and rigorous self-sufficiency which silently oozed aggression'.[3] According to this man, Graham had the capability to know right from wrong but had made a decision to ignore such considerations in order to satisfy his curious, perverted desires. Goodwill and genuine human warmth were not part of his make-up and never manifested themselves once. The only times he could be relied upon to tell the truth were when he described his indignation and self-pity at having been committed, or his enthusiasm for distasteful subjects such as Nazism and the British extreme right-wing groups. He hated any kind of discipline or authority, and regarded himself as utterly superior to any other person: 'One remembers his dry, chilling laugh coming from deep within his throat, invariably followed by a smirk of utter contempt.'[4]

After an initial rehabilitation period in a centre for ex-offenders, Graham managed to get himself a place to live in Hemel Hempstead, near Winifred's. His only psychiatric care consisted of three visits from a duty psychiatrist during his stay at the parole centre and two phone calls from Dr Udwin, who professed himself quite satisfied with Graham's progress, expressing the while his confidence that the man was no longer in any need of treatment of any kind.

The authorities took some care to protect Graham's anonymity and to hide the fact that he had spent most of his teenage years in a hospital for the criminally insane. It would be extremely difficult to evaluate this decision objectively, for had Graham actually been cured, his past, if known to others, would serve only to constantly hold him back and keep him ostracised from normal life. The opposing view, vindicated with the knowledge of hindsight, is that not allowing those he mixed with to realise the danger they might find themselves in robbed them of vital knowledge that could have saved lives.

Some of his colleagues at the resettlement centre later had their suspicions that Graham was up to his old tricks as soon as he was able to find a chemist shop. One of them recalled the 'tummy upsets' that went round, and a 'mystery bug' that nobody seemed to be able to get rid of. Even taking into account the understandable reasons for keeping his past secret, it does seem incredible that the halfway house he was sent to upon his release was left ignorant of Graham's criminal history.

In April 1971, a certain 'ME Evans' walked into a chemist's shop in London and asked for a quantity of antimony. He was refused, as he had no authority to purchase poisons. He appeared again a week later with the necessary papers, and was this time told all was in order. The young man gave an address in Willesden (near Graham's boyhood home of Neasden) and he signed the poisons register. This 'Mr Evans' had the air of being a medical student. He was scholarly in manner, and claimed to be involved in research. Having established the trust of the chemist, he came back yet again just under two weeks later, and bought more antimony and also some thallium. Graham Young was stocking up with his 'little friends' once again.

Another former inmate at the halfway house became friendly with Graham. Trevor Sparkes didn't seem to be a likely choice for a companion: he was an energetic sort who enjoyed playing football. Nevertheless the two of them began going to the pub together, and occasionally Graham would suggest they go back to his room and share a bottle of wine.

Sparkes paid the price soon afterwards when his legs became weak during a soccer match. On another occasion he started vomiting: Graham appeared to be very concerned about his friend and gave him a glass of water. Later Graham urged Sparkes to sip some wine, telling him that it might help his stomach. Needless to say, it didn't. His pains became unbearable and now included aching in his groin, constant sickness and more weakness in his muscles. His doctor thought a urinary infection was to blame but the prescribed drugs didn't help the problem.

Graham wasn't trying to kill Trevor Sparkes. He had administered what he later described as 'sub-lethal' doses of antimony. Mr Sparkes survived his dreadful ordeal, but Graham's administrations meant that he would never play football again.

In those days it was relatively easy to secure a job as long as you were prepared to accept whatever was offered. Graham managed to find employment at John Hadland's, a company that manufactured photographic lenses. He was to start as a storeman on a wage of £24 per week – perfectly acceptable in those days. In his letter of acceptance he wrote: 'May I take this opportunity to express my gratitude to you for offering me this position, notwithstanding my previous infirmity as communicated to you by the Placing Officer. I shall endeavour to justify your faith in me by performing my duties in an efficient and competent manner.'

By this time he had a bed-sitting room in Hemel Hempstead. His landlady and his fellow tenants had no idea at all that they were living with a former inmate of Broadmoor. His employers knew this much but had not been told why he had been sent there, and believed him to have been suffering from the after-effects of a nervous breakdown. They had a written report from Dr Udwin that stated Graham's suitability for the job, said that he was cured from what had ailed him, and made no mention of what the ailment had really been. Certainly no one knew, or could have known, about the mysterious Mr Evans and his 'research'.

It seemed to all and sundry that Graham had at last settled down. Although he seemed to be a rather strange person at times, there were plenty of people who were willing to offer the hand of friendship. He often visited his sister and the family, and made a regular habit of dining with them on Saturday evenings. It is almost certain that the reason these meals were left untampered with was only that Graham knew Winifred would be wise to him almost at once. If Graham was going to make any sort of comeback in his murderous career, he was going to have to make sure his victims were unsuspecting. There were plenty to choose from.

He couldn't resist indulging in small acts of bravado, and enjoyed the incredulous reactions that resulted. For instance, he paid a visit to one of his old neighbours in Neasden and, when they answered the door, asked innocently if they remembered him. He also went back to the chemist's where he had first managed to buy his poisons, and called on the headmaster who had been responsible for reporting him prior to his first arrest.

One might think he would have some antipathy towards these people, but he really didn't appear to; it was simply that he relished his notoriety, and needed to find ways of enjoying it without putting his longer-term plans at risk.

Meanwhile he was using Hadland's, his workplace, as his poison playground. Sometimes he merely toyed with his colleagues, sending them off to the lavatory with excruciating bouts of stomach-ache and vomiting. At other times, he chose to be more severe. The first of his workmates to actually die was the popular, robust chief storekeeper, Bob Egle. Mr Egle was 60, and had decided that it was about time to retire in order that he might enjoy what years of fitness he had left. When he felt a bit unwell in the early summer of 1971, his wife thought a holiday would be a good idea. It did the trick. Mr Egle went back to work thinking that whatever had caused his sickness had worked its way through his system. Only a day later, he lost all sensation in the ends of his fingers and had to come home from work once again. His appetite disappeared and he found that, when he tried to go out for a stroll, his legs wouldn't carry him. He spent the night in severe pain, and was extremely alarmed when his feet became as numb as his hands. He wasn't able to take the tablets the doctor gave him; he simply threw them up. He was admitted to hospital where the pain – mainly in his back – became even more severe.

Back at work, his young assistant was asking questions about how Mr Egle was faring, and what his symptoms were. When told that polyneuritis was suspected, he seemed to know all about the condition and voiced his concern.

Bob Egle was taken into intensive care, where he died at the beginning of July. The cause of death was listed as broncho-pneumonia brought about by polyneuritis. The workforce at Hadland's were shocked and extremely upset: he was well loved and his death was all the more tragic coming as it did at a time when he had been ready to enjoy retirement. The managing director decided the most politic course of action would be to represent the firm at Mr Egle's funeral by attending himself with the person who had recently been working most closely with the deceased. That other person was Bob Egle's former assistant: Graham Young.

On the way to and from the crematorium, Graham quizzed his boss about Bob's illness and asked what exactly had been diagnosed. He wasn't satisfied with 'polyneuritis', saying that the term was too general. Hadn't they given any more detail? The managing director couldn't remember anything, apart from that the condition had some sort of French-sounding name. Graham came up with the correct diagnosis straight away: 'Guillain-Barre Syndrome'. He went on, just as he always had done in the past, to impress his boss with a thorough knowledge of symptoms, effects, the state of research, and possible cures. He even explained that death had very likely been caused by broncho-pneumonia. His boss, who knew this was actually the case, was more than a little surprised.

Graham told his sister about Mr Egle's death and described it as having been the result of a 'strange virus'. He was continuing to flirt with discovery, either because he enjoyed the feeling of superiority it gave him over lesser mortals, or because he was so sure of himself that he thought he was unassailable. His sister thought he was quite genuine when he expressed his sadness at having been promoted to head of stores as a result of Mr Egle's death.

Graham carried on at work, always ready to fetch cups of tea or coffee from the drinks trolley that came round. Meanwhile, his colleagues were becoming extremely worried about the mysterious infection that seemed to be going round the building – and elsewhere. Ron Hewitt was the next one to fall seriously ill. He had acute pains in his throat and stomach, and kept vomiting. Not knowing what was afflicting them, the employees believed they were suffering from an unknown virus that had gone round their village once before: the 'Bovingdon Bug'. Mr Hewitt was lucky: he took a week off work and his illness miraculously cleared up. Fortunately for him, he later got himself another job, leaving Hadland's on the day of Mr Egle's funeral.

Peter Buck dealt with import and export at the company's laboratories. He had a relatively mild attack of the illness: he vomited and, unable to shake off his dreadful headache, was taken home by a clerk by the name of David Tilson. Mr Tilson, though, was not so lucky when the 'Bug' affected him. He went, for the umpteenth time, to see his doctor, who diagnosed possible thallium poisoning. As with others at Hadland's, Tilson's legs had become stiff and painful; he was having pins and needles in his feet; pains in the chest and stomach; difficulty in breathing, and his hair was falling out in handfuls. His doctor had come to the reasonable conclusion that, if poisoning was the cause of the problem, it was likely to be of an accidental nature. He asked Mr Tilson about any drugs he might be taking; he asked how much alcohol he drank; he checked for other possible causes, but all to no avail.

Meanwhile, colleague Jethro Batt, after he had commented on the bitter taste of the coffee, was asked by

Graham: 'What's the matter? Do you think I'm trying to poison you?' Mr Batt, a 39-year-old who had done his very best to befriend Graham, started with pains in his back and legs. Later, he began to retch terribly. He went home assuming that he was suffering from flu, but by the following Sunday his legs had gone completely numb. Four days later, the pains and the rigidity in his toes prevented him from rising from his bed. He was having hallucinations, and his hair began to fall out. He felt so wretched that he seriously considered ending his life.

Diana Smart (known as Di to everyone apart from Graham, who insisted on her full name) became mildly sick on two occasions and then, at the end of October, was sent home. Apart from what were now becoming distressingly familiar indications, she also had the problem of unpleasant foot odour. It was so bad that she had rows with her husband about it before he realised that the foul smell was not something his wife could do anything about.

Councillor Frederick Biggs was in charge of 'Works in Progress' at Hadland's. He was happy to help Graham in the main stores but had once pointed out, in a friendly enough way, that Graham might get into less of a muddle if he applied himself a bit more and didn't spend so much time wandering up and down, chatting and killing insects (he enjoyed doing both). This piece of friendly advice was eventually to mark Fred Biggs out as the next fatality. He was soon showing all the distressing signs, but Graham wanted to kill him in stages. During all this time, he had continued to play 'dare' with his colleagues. He was always willing to offer a plausible explanation for the illnesses, confident that nobody would discover just how he could be so knowledgeable about the matter, and he always asked about the invalids' progress. If people thought him over-concerned, they were correct. He most certainly was – but not for the reasons they supposed. His insistence on knowing exactly how much his victims were suffering was because this knowledge was vital to his experiments. Without it, his diary would be incomplete.

The 'diary' (as it became known) was found in Graham's bed-sit after his arrest. It was large and very detailed. He usually referred to his victims by one initial, e.g. B for Bob Egle; D was David Tilson; J was Jethro Batt; DI stood for Diana Smart; F for Fred Biggs, and so on. The following entries are those that his sister recorded. Though she never saw the diary herself, we can be sure the information is entirely accurate.

In the entry for 12 October, Graham described exactly how he intended to murder D (David Tilson) by visiting him in hospital, pretending to commiserate with him and then making a gift of a miniature bottle of uncontaminated brandy. This, of course, would be merely to lull the patient into a false sense of security so that the next time he was given the brandy, he would drink it without suspicion. The second bottle was to contain enough poison to bring Mr Tilson to the brink of death within a week – Graham predicted that he wouldn't be likely to survive much longer than that. The plan didn't work: Mr Tilson wasn't admitted to hospital until 20 October, and Graham commented: 'D has not been hospitalised – happy for him – and therefore is free to live out his allotted span. For needless to say it would be injudicious of me to focus my attention on him for a second time. I don't expect to see him for some time.'

R was a delivery driver from another firm. He was, according to the notes, 'an ideal subject'. The friendly storekeeper at Hadland's was always available for a chat, and a cup of tea: 'He should visit this week and the chance will appear then,' Graham wrote. 'This time I must restrain my tendency to over-liberal doses.' His 'tendency to over-liberal doses' was to be avoided for no other reason than the importance Graham placed upon observing the slowed-down effects of smaller ones.

He did feel remorse, albeit with certain reservations. Again referring to R, he wrote: 'In a way it seems a shame to condemn such a likeable man to such a horrible end, but I have made my decision and therefore he is doomed to premature decease.'

He was even more regretful in the case of Jethro Batt. Regarding 18 October he wrote: 'A second development and one which I now regret, is that J has been afflicted.' And later on, he recorded that he now felt '. . . rather ashamed of my action in harming Jeth. I think he is a really nice fellow and the nearest to a friend I have at Hadland's. I have faith he will recover.'

This was, of course, extremely unusual for him and we do not know what prompted these uncharacteristic twinges of conscience. Although his victims were 'not people' as far as he was concerned, it seems that he did sometimes decide their fates because of some petty ideas of revenge. It didn't need to be much: a cross word, a bit of teasing – to Graham the death sentence was applicable to anybody who vexed him: 'DI irritated me intensely yesterday, so I packed her off home with an attack of sickness. I only gave her something to shake her up. I now regret I didn't give her a larger dose capable of laying her up for a few days.'

On 31 October he wrote of Councillor Fred Biggs: 'I have administered a fatal dose of the special compound to him and anticipate a report of his progress on

Monday, 1 November.' Later he wrote: 'F is now seriously ill. He is unconscious and it is likely that he will decline in the next few days. It will be a merciful release for him as, if he should survive, he will be permanently impaired. It is better that he should die. It will remove one more casualty from the crowded field of battle.' And later still: 'F must have phenomenal strength . . . If he lives it could be inconvenient. It is better he should die. Too many health authorities are becoming involved for me to press the matter further.'

The final entry in the diary referred to 'latest news from the hospital' with regard to F. It said F was responding to treatment and added, 'He is surviving far too long for my peace of mind.'

If there were any suspicions about Graham, they were no more than mild misgivings, brought about by his unusual attitude. When Mrs Smart went to the managing director with her worries, she had to be satisfied with the explanation she was given: that anything odd about Graham was probably the result of the 'nervous breakdown' he had suffered prior to his arrival. That did indeed explain things away, and Diana Smart went back to work, still a little dubious but attributing her misgivings to Graham's lesser idiosyncrasies. The illnesses, meanwhile, were no longer thought to be connected to any kind of virus: they must have a less abstruse basis. In the end, it was suspected that the firm had a Health and Safety issue to deal with. This became urgent on Friday 19 November 1971, when the death of Councillor Fred Biggs was announced. On the same day a memo was circulated, asking the entire staff to attend a meeting at which the company's in-house doctor, Arthur Anderson, would address them.

In fact, Dr Anderson didn't have very much to say. He was as baffled as everyone else but he did his very best to reassure the company that everything was being done to eliminate the dreadful sickness which, he thought, had several possible causes including contamination by radioactive material. The building and materials used had all been thoroughly checked, he told them, and there was absolutely no danger from anything they had to work with. He then invited questions from members of the workforce.

Graham Young certainly did have questions. To the doctor's immense astonishment, he began by asking whether any of the symptoms were consistent with thallium poisoning. In fact, Dr Anderson had considered this very possibility, but had chosen not to voice his fears in order to avoid panic. He never suspected that, in the present case, thallium was deliberately being admixed with food and drink: he thought, rather, that the likelihood was that it was being used in the firm's production of camera lenses. He had investigated this possibility, and found that Hadland's did not stock thallium at all. The poison need not be orally imbibed for it to do its damage: it can be absorbed through the skin. The thought was horrific, and not any less worrying now that Anderson was faced with a man who appeared to know all about this obscure toxin.

He tried to curtail Graham's thoroughgoing lecture on the neurological damage thallium could cause. Anderson didn't know very much about its effects himself, but he was astute enough to be aware that this kind of speech would not help matters at all. When he finally managed to shut Graham up, he brought the meeting to a close. However, he had to acknowledge to himself that Graham had been quite correct: the symptoms did suggest thallium poisoning. Some time before the meeting, John Hadland, the company chairman, and Godfrey Foster, the managing director, had come to the conclusion, astonishing though it seemed to them, that they had to suspect malicious practice.

Graham simply had to be the first person they looked towards. His bragging about poisons and chemicals and his general behaviour singled him out. Before the meeting, his bosses had therefore decided that the time had come to call in the police. As he had done all those years before with his school psychiatrist, Graham, by the nature of his responses, incriminated himself more and more. The two men agreed to wait until Dr Anderson had had time for a private chat with Graham.

Like so many before him, Anderson was awestruck by the man's wide-ranging knowledge of chemistry, but noted that it related only to poisons, and not to the wider matters that, say, a medical student would have been acquainted with. Knowing Graham's medical history and the fact that Graham had once been an inmate of Broadmoor, Anderson had to agree with Hadland and Foster: Graham Young was their most likely suspect.

The police arrested him at his Aunt Win's house in Sheerness, Kent, at 11.30 p.m. on 20 November. He wasn't quite as nonchalant about the charges as he had been when he was a schoolboy. According to his aunt, he went white. Trembling with shock, she asked him what he'd been up to now. He said he didn't know – he had no idea what the they were talking about. On the way to the police station, Graham asked the arresting officer, 'Which one is it for?'

He was not willing to confess, as he had been previously. When asked about the incriminating diary, he said it was fictional – notes for a novel he was intending to write. He told the arresting officers that they would have to work hard to prove a case against him: they would have to identify the poisons they alleged he had administered; prove that he had had an opportunity to do it, and then come up with some sort of motive. He doubted they would be able to do any of this, and was absolutely certain that the last criterion couldn't possibly be fulfilled. Underneath all this, he must have known that he would be found guilty in the end. Frank Jones, in his book *Murderous Innocents*, puts forward the very plausible supposition that Graham was reluctant to deny himself the glory of a full trial.

He had been preparing himself for the possibility of being discovered but, if his diary is to be believed, he had a scenario in mind very different from the one that actually came about. On 3 November he had noted that the hospital had come to the conclusion that D's [Mr Tilson's] total loss of hair had been caused by poisoning. 'I must watch the situation very carefully,' he had written. 'If it looks like I will be detected then I shall have to destroy myself. The events of the next few days will prove decisive. They will point either to my continuation to live or my destruction by my own hand.' He had taken to carrying with him a phial of thallium which, he told the police, was his 'exit dose'. He explained that he hadn't had any opportunity to use it yet, as he hadn't anticipated being arrested in Sheerness. He was later to deny this in court, saying that had he intended to commit suicide, he possessed other chemicals that would have killed him far more quickly than thallium could.

Graham Young's trial, commencing on 19 June 1972, lasted ten days. He was found guilty on all the major charges. Lesser counts of administering poison could not be proven. His counsel explained that Graham had been at liberty to commit his more recent crimes only because of his release from Broadmoor. This had been a serious error of judgement, and the Court now had a duty to protect Graham from himself, as well as to protect the public from him. Should the judge be considering sending him back to a mental institution instead of to prison, Graham himself expressed a wish to go to prison. Ever objective about his own condition, it would, he thought, be the more effective alternative.

His sister, Winifred, stood by him, and went on to write her detailed and honest book abut Graham's life and crimes. She later developed cancer, and died at the age of 43. Fred Young was to follow her soon afterwards. He was never reconciled with his son. Graham himself died in the late summer of 1990. He had apparently suffered a heart attack at the age of 43. In 1996, a film was made of his life. *The Young Poisoner's Handbook* is listed in video stores as a comedy.

4. THE WORLD'S WORST

'It's not her fault she grew up this way; it's not her fault she was born.'[1]

The barrister who made this comment had not been the legal advocate for the child in question and what he said was generally ignored. The eleven-year-old girl was demonised and condemned by both the press and the public, neither wanting to hear anything that contradicted their prejudice. Yet in truth it wasn't her fault that she grew up in the way she did. If anyone was to blame, it was her mother.

We don't know the reason or reasons for the mother's antipathy towards little May (as she was known to her family). It may have been because she was illegitimate. In the north of England in 1957, the shame that followed giving birth to a 'bastard' would envelop both mother and baby wherever they went. For the mother, this burden would be in addition to the obvious problems that go with being a single parent, without any reliable means of support. May's mother, Betty, would never reveal who the father was. One thing was clear: little May's arrival had had little to do with romance, or love. When she was first presented with her baby, Betty rejected her emphatically. Her words were chilling, and now seem to hang over May's life like a curse: 'Take that thing away from me!'

Betty married a year later and her new husband, Billy, though something of a ne'er-do-well, became – to all intents and purposes – the little girl's father. A second child was born – a boy – and the family moved in with Betty's mother in Gateshead, near Newcastle. It wasn't long before Betty tried to harm her baby daughter.

May was only one year old when her grandmother found that she'd eaten some pills. She was taken to hospital and recovered without any lasting damage. How she'd managed to reach the pills, and why she'd eaten them, remained something of a mystery. The bottle was kept in the back of an old gramophone player in a box, which in turn was in a drawer; the machine itself stood on a small chest. To get into the drawer required an implement of some kind (May's grandmother used a knitting needle). The pills themselves were not pleasant to the taste and it seemed incredible that a small child should want to chew them. However, that – apparently – was what had happened.

If there were suspicions, they were not acted upon. Betty's relationship with her daughter was hardly a loving one, but it wasn't until she began to try to rid herself of the child in other, more obvious ways that her family intervened.

Betty had a sister called Cath who, in turn, was friendly with a couple who had always liked May very much and who had previously offered to look after the baby on a permanent basis if her responsibilities should ever prove too much. In November 1959, Betty wrote to Cath, announcing that she had given May into the couple's keeping. Cath was horrified when she heard this (though had she known what May's life with Betty was to be, she might have seen the turn of events as providential: it could have been the child's deliverance from a dreadful fate). In the event, Cath took May back to Betty at once, thereby unwittingly robbing the child of an opportunity to have a normal life.

When May was nearly three, Cath found her and her little brother eating what she first imagined were the sweets that she'd brought for them earlier. Then she noticed that there were pills mingled with the 'dolly mixtures'. Panic-stricken, she grabbed the children, and made them drink salt water in order to make them vomit. The pills were Drinamyls, or 'purple hearts', and they belonged to Betty. She insisted that she was not to blame for what had happened. She said she kept them in her handbag at all times and that the children must have managed to get at them when she wasn't looking. Again, there were suspicions: why would they steal pills when there were sweets to eat? How, in any case, had the children managed it?

Cath and her husband must have realised that to leave May with Betty was dangerous. In spite of having 'rescued' her from prospective adoptive parents, they suggested that they themselves should look after the baby permanently. Despite her manifest desire to rid herself of the responsibilities of motherhood, Betty refused.

Not long afterwards, May nearly fell out of a window. Luckily, her uncle managed to grab her before she actually fell. This incident may possibly have been the result of carelessness, but the rest of the family resolved to make sure that Betty was no longer left alone with her child.

Just a few days afterwards, Betty changed her mind again. This time, she took the child to an adoption agency. Before they had been seen, a distressed, would-be adoptive mother emerged from an unsuccessful interview, age counting against her, as did the fact that she was about to move to Australia. Betty thrust May at her with the words: 'I brought this one in to be adopted.

You can have her.' She left her child with the stranger, and went home.

May's Aunt Isa was able to follow the woman and to find out where she lived. She told May's grandmother what had happened and, for the third time in her young life, May was brought back to her mother. She remembered the house where the woman had taken her, and the new dresses she'd been bought. She remembers her aunt coming to take her back and she was to wonder, years later, why her aunt had done that: 'Why didn't they leave me with that lady who wanted a child?'

May, still only a toddler, was in hospital again. She had had her stomach pumped after swallowing iron-supplement pills – 'Smarties', she called them – which, she said, her mother had given her. Betty tearfully denied having done any such thing. She *had* done it, though: one of May's little friends had seen her do it. The family didn't believe Betty's protestations and the incident created a year-long rift between them. Away from the protection of her aunts and grandmother, the child was at the mercy of her mother's erratic and abusive behaviour. It was during this time that the dreadful sexual abuse began.

Money was a constant difficulty. Betty's husband Billy, a sometime thief, was rarely at home, and she often earned extra cash by selling sexual favours. Paradoxically, she was also a fervent – though unconventional – Roman Catholic who kept a room full of crucifixes and rosaries. Her sexual life was something she felt ashamed of but which (to be charitable) was one of the very few ways by which she could put food on the table. May remembers a time when she walked in on her mother and the landlord, just as he was doing his trousers up: Betty had been 'paying the rent'. She was livid at being found out and, yanking her child by the hair, she threw her into the scullery.

If Betty had done this because of shame, or even out of a warped protective instinct, such feelings didn't stand in her way when she found out that her four-year-old (or maybe five-year-old) daughter was of interest to her clients. Betty would hold May and, keeping the child's arms pinioned behind her, force her head back by pulling her hair. Then the man would put his penis in the little girl's mouth. When he ejaculated, May vomited.

This was not an isolated incident. There were times when Betty would 'play Blind Man's Buff', putting a stocking over May's eyes before turning her round and making her perform oral sex. She would put something in May's mouth: 'a silky thing to . . . to keep my mouth open and it was so dreadful, with the rosaries you know, bumping into me you know. I felt so bad, so bad.'

Betty told May that if she said anything about these goings-on, she would be put away. She pointed out a sentry box on the Tyne Bridge and said that that was where she would be locked up; no one would believe her stories, anyway.

She never did tell – not until after her mother's death, when she confided in the writer Gitta Sereny. The result was the book *Cries Unheard*. May's real name has become notorious. Ms Sereny's book was the first comprehensive account of the terrible childhood that drove her to kill two small boys. She is – or was, then – Mary Bell.

Mary grew up into what the courts would see as a manipulative, cunning girl. Had anybody known how this had come about, she might have been afforded a lot more sympathy than she received. Scotswood, where she was living at the time her name became public, was a closely-knit, working-class community in Newcastle. It was then a depressed area with high unemployment but, generally, people looked out for their neighbours and it was a friendly enough environment. Children played, without fear of molestation, on the wasteland and in the streets: no one would have seriously considered that their child might be at risk. There were accidents, of course – and there were places the kids were told to stay away from. On 11 May 1968, a three-year-old cousin of Mary's, John Best, 'fell' some several feet down an embankment behind some empty sheds. He sustained cuts to his head. Mary and her friend Norma raised the alarm and John was taken to the nearby Delaval Arms public house. He said he'd been pushed, but wouldn't say who'd done it. The police decided that the incident had been accidental.

Mary was a bully. She was a pretty child: small, dark and with blue eyes. Her friendships with other children were few and far between, but the one with Norma had endured. They had met at the beginning of 1967 when, shortly after the Bells moved into Whitehouse Road, another family moved in next door. The second household were also called Bell, but they were not related. The newcomers' household, with eleven children, was a livelier set than Mary's family. She used to wonder how on·earth they all managed in such a small space (apparently they had their meals in shifts). Mary's previous best friend had moved away and when Susan Bell suggested she and Mary play together, Mary was happy to accept. Susan turned out to be too straight-laced for Mary's liking: she was always complaining and never misbehaved. Mary preferred the company of Susan's elder sister, Norma.

Norma and Mary lived for the next few months in a childhood wonderland of adventure and imaginary deeds of 'derring-do'. They would dream up scenarios such as prison breakouts or stories involving American outlaws like Jesse James and his gang.

Mary, particularly, had a warped sense of morality, which was the result of her experience and upbringing. Her stepfather would refer to burglaries and petty thievery as 'work', while her mother never spoke of any figure of authority without using the word 'fucking' in the same breath. The two girls would egg each other on to do things which were at times quite dangerous; at others they were simply naughty. Once dared, Mary would always rise to the challenge. Norma was slightly less fond of these games, but she also was something of a trouble-maker. She frequently got into fights, many of them with black children. It wasn't clear where this dislike of children from other races had come from, but it was certainly there. The older Mary told Gitta Sereny that while she, Mary, was misbehaving in a misguided attempt to assert herself as a person who didn't need her family, Norma, overshadowed as she was by her many siblings, was probably getting into trouble so that her family would actually take more notice of her.

Norma had also run away from home more than once: '. . . she kept saying she hated home, she wanted to be away from them. Much later I wondered whether they ever noticed when she ran away . . . Now that I think of it, she was also often . . . I don't know . . . just sad. I think we were both, in our own way, very sad little girls'.[2]

The day after Mary's cousin's 'accident', the police were contacted again, this time by the mother of Pauline Watson, a seven-year-old girl who had been bullied by two older children. Pauline had said one of them had tried to strangle her. She had been playing in a sandpit with two of her friends when the older girls had arrived. One of them had told Pauline to get out of the pit, but she had refused. The girl had then put her hands around Pauline's neck and squeezed – she had then done the same to one of the other little ones.

Mary and Norma were identified as the culprits and, when questioned, each blamed the other. Norma said, after this, that she wasn't a friend of Mary's any more.

It was only a couple of weeks later that the body of Martin Brown was discovered in a derelict house. The little boy (he was four years old) was lying on the floor, with blood and saliva running from his mouth. The group of boys that found him saw Mary and Norma climbing through a window into the building next door. They told the girls to go away, but Mary brushed them aside. Full of a sense of her own importance, she declared: 'It's all right, the police know I'm here.' When the boys still wouldn't let them through, it was Mary and Norma who, unbidden, went to tell Martin's aunt that the boy had had an accident. Later they offered to play with her son John. They both acted strangely, grinning all the time and asking inappropriate questions: 'Do you miss Martin?' 'Do you cry for him?' 'Does June [Martin's mother] miss him?'[3]

Four days after his death, Mary called on June and, smiling in a strange way, asked if she could see Martin. Thinking the girl was in some way unable to comprehend the finality of death, June tried to explain: 'No, pet. Martin's dead.' Grinning, Mary replied, 'Oh, I know he's dead. I wanted to see him in his coffin.'[4]

On 26 May, a Sunday, which also happened to be Mary's eleventh birthday, the Woodlands Crescent

Nursery was vandalised. The damage was mainly superficial but, along with the chaos of ruined artwork, provisions and cleaning materials, were four notes. It seemed as if they had been written by two different children, each supplying alternate letters. They read:

I murder SO That I may come back

fuch of
we murder
watch out
Fanny and FAggot

WE did murder Martain brown,
fuckof you BAstArd

YOU ArE micey y BecuaSe we murderd Martain GO
Brown you BettER Look out THErE arE MurdErs
about by FANNYAND and auld Faggot you srcews[5]

On the same day that these notes were discovered, Mary wrote about Martin's death in her schoolbook:

On Saturday I was in the house, and my mam sent Me
to ask Norma if she Would come up the top with me?
We went up and we came down at Magrets Road and
there were crowds of people beside an old house. I
asked what was the matter. There had been a boy who
Just lay down and Died.[6]

Beneath the writing was a picture of Martin's body (positioned accurately and with the word 'TABLET' next to it showing where an empty pill bottle had been found near him). Beside this she'd drawn a picture of a workman in a cloth cap, with some kind of pick over his shoulder. Her teacher didn't attach any significance to her work; the notes were assumed to be a childish joke and were filed away without much further investigation. The nursery was cleaned up and an alarm was fitted.

A week later, the nursery's new burglar alarm went off: Mary and Norma were caught breaking in. They wouldn't admit to the previous incident and, after being given a date to appear before a juvenile court, they were released into the custody of their parents.

Mary's troubled mind was causing her to lash out in all directions. She even attacked Norma, scratching her and kicking her in the eye. She shouted out 'I am a murderer!' and '. . . that house over there, that's where I killed . . . Brown.'[7] A boy, who witnessed this outburst, didn't take her seriously: Mary was always boasting about something or other.

The rift between the two girls healed quickly and the next day, a Saturday, they ran away together. Their escapade only lasted until the Sunday, but a fortnight later they tried again. The second time they managed to get much further and were not picked up for two days. Mary was punished by her mother on both occasions and the authorities did not pursue the matters. When, eventually, social workers did call to enquire into Mary's background, Betty refused to have them in the house.

A short time after this, Brian Howe, another toddler, was found dead. It was on 31 July 1968, the same year, and it was plain that the death of the three-year-old was definitely not an accident.

Brian, a golden-haired little boy in good health, lived at 64 Whitehouse Road. His mother had left the family home, but his father, helped by his fourteen-year-old sister Pat and his elder brother's girlfriend Irene, managed to provide a loving home.

Earlier that day, Brian and his friend John had been found by the derelict houses in St Margaret's Road. Rita, John's mother, was angry when she saw the toddlers so near to these buildings, which were in a dangerous condition. The tragic death of Martin Brown had been blamed on the fact that the structures ought not to have been left standing so long. Afterwards, there had been protests and petitions. Now, workmen were gradually demolishing the block. She shouted in anger at the workmen, and smacked the children. She later sent her son John to bed and told Brian to go home; to tell his mother where he'd been, and to tell her that he'd already been smacked for it.

Brian preferred to go off to play, which is what he did. Children remembered seeing him in the street during that afternoon. He'd been with his brother and a couple of girls on bicycles (not Mary and Norma). When Pat called him in for his 'tea' at five o'clock, he wasn't anywhere to be seen. Pat asked Mary Bell, who was sitting on a doorstep nearby, whether she had seen him. Mary willingly offered to help look for the missing boy. Not very long afterwards, Norma joined in the hunt. There was no great panic – it was generally assumed that Brian had wandered off by himself and would turn up before long.

They went to all the usual places: the local sweet shop; a car park where the kids sometimes played; and then over to the sprawling wasteland known locally as 'the Tin Lizzie', but there was no sign of Brian. Mary pointed to some huge slabs of concrete and wondered aloud whether Brian might have been playing near them and fallen. Norma intervened quickly: 'Oh no,' she said. 'He never goes there.' Pat agreed; they didn't bother to investigate.

It was seven o'clock and Brian hadn't been seen since the afternoon. The search party made a final check of the park; then Pat, decidedly anxious by this time, said she was going to call the police.

The police searched throughout the evening, using artificial lights. They found Brian's body just after eleven o'clock.

It was near to where Mary had suggested he might have fallen.

He was fully dressed and had been covered in grass and the purple flowers that grew all over the Tin Lizzie. His arm was stretched out, his lips had turned blue and he had the characteristic marks of strangulation on his neck. His body had several light stab wounds including, it was later discovered, cuts to the genitals. A pair of broken scissors lay nearby.

It was assumed that a perverted adult had killed Brian after a sexual assault, but this theory didn't hold for long. The tentative way in which the cuts had been inflicted strongly suggested that they were the work of a child. For the next eight days, the people of Scotswood were questioned by the police; questionnaires were sent to every house and over a thousand children were interviewed.

Detective Constable Kerr remembered the difference between the two Bell families on Whitehouse Road. He first went to Norma's, where the concerned reaction was similar to what he might have expected – although, as he told Gitta Sereny: 'I did think Norma was peculiar. I mean, I was enquiring into something pretty awful and little Brian was a child they had all known well, but there she was continually smiling as if it was a huge joke. Her mother – and I thought that was odd, too, under the circumstances – was quite sharp with her: "Didn't you hear what he asked? Answer the question!" '[8]

Asked what she had been doing that day, Norma at first failed to mention that she had seen Mary Bell at all. She mentioned two other children with whom she'd been making pom-poms. This transpired to be the truth – but not, by any means, all of it.

On calling next door, he was struck by the lack of emotional warmth: 'It was a very different atmosphere in there. No feeling of a home whatever, just a shell: very peculiar, no sound, beat-up furniture and very little of it, and airless, stuffy, dark, you know, on a brilliant summer afternoon. The only life one felt was the barking of a big dog, a ferocious-looking Alsatian.'[9]

Mary was evasive in manner, and her stepfather – the only adult about – behaved oddly. He said he was Mary's uncle and that her mother was away on business. This lie about his relationship to the child had a less culpable explanation than Kerr would have been interested in. Betty was claiming social security benefits as a single parent, and had been passing Billy off as Mary's uncle for some time.

It was Mary herself, though, who was the object of DC Kerr's attention. She said, more or less, the same as Norma had: that they had seen Brian Howe in the road outside at about half past twelve on 31 July. She said she hadn't been near the Tin Lizzie for over two months.

Children are not usually very good at keeping up a lie. The inconsistencies soon become evident and a desire to elaborate overrides their ability to sound convincing. When Norma was questioned again, she added to her account an admission that she had been with Mary that afternoon from 2.30 p.m. They had not left the immediate vicinity of Whitehouse Road together, but had parted at about 5 p.m. 'As far as I know,' Norma wrote, 'Mary . . . just went into her house.'[10]

Mary's story also changed in small details and, gradually, things were mentioned that she ought not to have known if she had been telling the truth. She tried to implicate an eight-year-old local boy whom she'd seen (she said) covered in grass and purple flowers. She'd seen this boy hit Brian for no apparent reason. He'd been playing with a pair of broken scissors and he'd tried to cut off a cat's tail with them. The police immediately thought they were onto something: the scissors had not been mentioned in any of the press reports. However, when they checked, they found that the boy in question had spent the day at Newcastle Airport, some eight miles away. Mary's statement was still important, but now it told them something completely different from their first supposition. If she was not the killer herself, Mary Bell must have at least seen Brian's body before its discovery: she certainly knew more about his death than she was telling them.

By Sunday 4 August, the police had eliminated everyone but the two Bell girls. Meanwhile, guilt or fear had had their effect on Norma. She broke down in tears and asked to talk without her father being present. Although the absence of a responsible adult could have rendered her statement inadmissible, her father left the room before the officer could stop him. What she intended to say was still only a version of the truth but it was closer to what had actually happened than anything either girl had said before. That afternoon, on 31 July, Mary had told her she was going to take her 'to see Brian . . .' The officer asked her to stop talking for a while: he needed this to be official.

Later at the police station, with her father present, she was interviewed by Chief Inspector Dobson and two other officers. After being cautioned, she went on with her story, saying Mary had taken her down to the 'blocks' (the concrete slabs where Brian had been found). She had tripped over the dead boy's head. Mary had told her she'd strangled him: 'I squeezed his neck and pushed up his lungs, that's how you kill them.' She had told Norma she must 'keep her nose dry and not tell anyone.'[11] Mary had then produced a razor blade from where it was hidden nearby and shown Norma where she'd cut Brian's belly. At this point, no such lacerations had been noticed on the body, but Norma was able to take the police to the place where the razor was still hidden. She also demonstrated exactly the position in which the body had been found.

She later gave a statement:

. . . He was lying on his back and his left arm was out by his side with the palm up, it was covered with black dirt. May said, 'Keep your nose dry, he's dead.' I could see his head and nearly all his jersey. It was a red pattern. His legs were covered with grass. Round his lips were purple. May touched his lips and his nose, there was a funny mark on his nose. His eyes were open. I knew he was dead by his face. She got hold of my neck under the chin and said that was how she had done it, by squeezing his lungs up and she enjoyed doing it. She said she took him there to harm him.[12]

Norma was taken to a council-run children's home for girls in Newcastle and the officer in charge, Chief Inspector Dobson, and two of his constables went back to Whitehouse Road to interview Mary Bell. It was by now just after midnight.

The television was on and, despite the hot weather, there was a fire roaring away. Mary was in bed, asleep, and at first Billy refused to wake her. Mr Dobson explained that it was a matter of urgency and it would be better for Mary if he (Billy) woke her rather than a policeman but, if he continued to stand in their way, they would do what they had to. Billy told them to wait while he went across the road to get Mary's Aunt Audrey.

It was Audrey who came with them to the police station, not Billy. She put a protective arm around Mary and told her she must tell the truth. Mary, who might have been expected to be alarmed by her predicament, was quite spirited and didn't seem at all put out.

She said she hadn't been to the concrete blocks on the Tin Lizzie that day – she had only been there once before and that was a long time ago. Of course she denied Norma's accusations and, when she was told that a man had seen the two of them running away, she replied, 'He would have to have good eyesight.' Mr Dobson picked her up on it immediately: it perhaps showed she knew more about the area than she was letting on. 'Why would he need good eyesight?'

Mary was quick – very quick – but there was a slight pause while she worked out a suitable reply: 'Because he was . . . clever to see me when I wasn't there.'[13]

She then said she was going home and when told that she couldn't, she accused them of brainwashing her. Mr Dobson made an oblique reference to the razor blade, saying that Norma had told them Mary had hidden 'something' which they now had in their possession. 'What was it?' Mary demanded. 'I'll kill her.'[14]

It was a long, slow interview. Mary often jumped up and said she was going home. She wouldn't keep still and sometimes sat for long intervals while questions were repeated to her. When Mr Dobson's phone rang, she asked him if the office was bugged. She did, however, keep to her story: she knew nothing about Brian's death and Norma was lying. What she asserted wasn't impossible and there was no actual evidence to connect her to the killing. She was sent home in the early hours of the morning.

Norma Bell's next statement – her fourth – was different yet again. Every part of what she had said earlier was true, she insisted, but there was something else that she was keen to tell them. She had been with Mary earlier and had gone with her and little Brian to the concrete blocks on the Tin Lizzie. They had with them a pair of scissors that Brian's brother had given to the little boy. They had climbed inside an old tank, which was smelly, and they all got out again almost immediately. It was after that that Mary had told Brian to lift his neck.

She got him down on the grass and she seemed to go all funny, you could tell there was something the matter with her. She kept on struggling with him and he was struggling and trying to get her hands away. She let go of him and I could hear him gasping. She squeezed his neck again and I said, 'May, leave the baby alone', but she wouldn't. She said to me, 'My hands are getting thick, take over.' Then I ran away. I went back the way we had come.[15]

Norma said she had gone back to Whitehouse Road and played with some other kids. Twenty minutes later, Mary had arrived and told her to go back with her to the Tin Lizzie. The rest of her previous statement was the truth: she *had* tripped over Brian's head and Mary *had* confessed to strangling him. Mary had taken a razor blade and made marks on Brian's belly. They had gone back home and at about five o'clock, just after Mary had emerged from her early evening meal, they had gone back yet again. This is when Mary had stabbed him with the scissors. She had also said that she wanted to make Brian 'baldy' and she had cut some of his hair away 'at the front'.

The body was re-examined and this time they found something new. A razor blade had been used to cut a deliberate pattern into his belly. It could have been begun as a letter 'N' but had been added to and now formed an 'M'. The marks had not been visible before, but decomposition had brought them into view. It is entirely possible that the marks, like the notes found in the vandalised nursery, had been made by two different hands.

Two days later, Brian was buried. There was a huge turnout at the funeral. Chief Inspector Dobson was watching Mary very carefully. He saw her standing in front of the Howes' house. As the tiny coffin was brought out, she laughed and rubbed her hands together. He now realised that Norma's statement was substantially true. With a sudden feeling of dread, he realised that this child was dangerous and that he had to arrest her before she killed again.

Mary's subsequent statement tallied with much of what Norma had told them, except that she reversed the roles of perpetrator and onlooker:

> . . . *Brian started to cry and Norma asked him if he had a sore throat. She started to squeeze his throat and he started to cry . . . Norma says, 'Put your neck up,'*

and he did. Then she got hold of his neck and said 'Put it down.' She started to feel up and down his neck. She squeezed it hard, you could tell it was hard because her fingertips were going white. Brian was struggling, and I was pulling her shoulders but she went mad. I was pulling her chin up but she screamed at me. By this time she had banged Brian's head on some wood or corner of wood and Brian was lying senseless. His face was all white and bluey and his eyes were open. His lips were purplish and had all like slaver on, it turned into something like fluff. Norma covered him up and I said, 'Norma, I've got nothing to do with this, I should tell on you, but I'll not.'

She went on to describe the mutilation of the body, with Norma as the villain of the piece and she, Mary, the worried, frightened and helpless witness:

. . . she [Norma] says "May, you shouldn't have done it 'cos you'll get into trouble", and I hadn't done nothing I haven't got the guts. I couldn't kill a bird by the neck or throat or anything, it's horrible that.[16]

The police were already making the connections between Brian Howe's death and Martin Brown's. For the present, they decided to concentrate on the former. Both girls were told that they were being charged with the little boy's murder. Norma cried out, 'I never, you know.' Earlier, Mary's response had been, 'That's all right with me.'

The two children were taken into custody. Their first night was spent at Newcastle police station in cells specially intended for juvenile offenders. Mary was pleased that she had been given fish and chips for supper. She couldn't sleep: she was worried that she might wet the bed. 'I usually do,' she told the woman police officer who was guarding them. She sat there, in the growing light, about to be taken to court to face a murder charge, and she sang:

Oh you are a mucky kid,
Dirty as a dustbin lid
When he hears the things you did
You'll get a belt from your Da[17]

Mary's comments to those who were appointed to look after her during her trip to Seaham Remand Home, and the psychiatrists who examined her afterwards, all testified to her inability to comprehend the enormity of what she had done. She was worried that Betty might have to pay a fine; she hoped her mother wouldn't be 'too upset'. 'Brian Howe had no mother,' she said, 'so he won't be missed.' When asked whether she knew how it would feel to be strangled, she said in an off-hand manner: 'Why? If you're dead, you're dead. It doesn't matter then.' During her trial, she told a policewoman: 'Murder isn't that bad. We all die some-time anyway.'[18]

Whereas journalists of today would have little compunction in depicting the two defendants in terms as lurid as possible, those of the late 1960s saw their subject matter as rather distasteful and one to be reported without too much detail. The reporters were much in evidence, though: extra seats had been made available for them in anticipation of huge media interest. Large numbers of the public were also expected, but they didn't come. When Betty and Billy Bell, together with a friend of theirs who was evidently acting as some ghastly version of a literary agent, offered Mary's story to the Sunday papers, they were disappointed: the reporter felt sickened by their attitude and when the couple's friend rang the London office, they told him that they 'wouldn't touch it with a ten-foot pole'. The gold-diggers were sent away empty-handed.

Over the next few weeks, despite this astonishing restraint, the image of Mary Bell as a demon child grew steadily. Norma, on the other hand, was viewed very much in the way she had put herself forward in her statement: as the essentially innocent friend who had simply had the misfortune to come under the influence of a heartless psychopath.

That there should be two different perceptions was not surprising: neither child was at all aware of how their conduct in court would affect public sympathy but, whereas Norma elicited sympathy, Mary did not. Gitta Sereny was one of the few people present to pick up on the almost imperceptible signs of Mary's inner confusion.

She described the differences between the two girls in both of her books about the case. Norma behaved very much as one might expect a child to behave: she was clearly terrified, quite out of her depth and extremely distressed. She wasn't able fully to follow the proceedings, while Mary, on the other hand, appeared to take in every detail. Mary wasn't overawed; she showed no terror, or obvious discomfiture; she could even have been enjoying the whole thing. Ms Sereny noticed her constant hand movements as she stroked her dress, sucked her finger, or wiped her mouth.

Norma was supported throughout by her family, who sat behind her, always ready to offer comfort when the ordeal overwhelmed her and provoked tears. Mary, although she had the reassuring presence of her grandmother and aunts, had to cope with her mother's public demonstrations of her own distress. Betty wept, protested and generally drew attention to herself. She often walked out of court, apparently too indignant to face any more of the drama. If she did ever offer comfort to her child, she did it for effect, when she knew she was being observed.

The surroundings in which the trial was held were set up with the intention of it being as discreet and as accommodating to the needs of the children as possible. The room was a relatively small one and the baying mob that a present-day Norma and Mary might expect was nowhere to be seen. Mary's private attitude to the accusations was revealed years later. She told Ms Sereny that she found the whole thing unreal.

'I didn't *know* I had intended for them to be dead . . . dead for ever. Dead for me then wasn't for ever.' In an attempt to define exactly what she meant by this, she recalled how her dog had died 'two or three times I think'. On each occasion, her stepfather had replaced the animal and all had carried on as before. She had a vague feeling that she would be hanged, but didn't connect the concept to any fear concerning her own death. She said that it didn't mean anything that was real to her. During that same interview (for *Cries Unheard*) she acknowledged that the court wanted her to show some sort of regret about what she had done. She couldn't do this, she remembered, because she hadn't comprehended then what she actually *had* done. In the way that many children do when they are in any sort of trouble, she could only persist in the lies she had told, and try to make them as convincing as possible.

This inability to understand her predicament, the apparent callousness that resulted from it and Mary's

frozen emotional state are largely responsible for her continuing notoriety. Had she broken down and wept, had she shown fear, she might have gained enough sympathy for the case to be consigned to history, and forgotten much earlier. Her apparent cold-heartedness – her 'cannyness' – was to give rise to the myth of Mary Bell. Even years later, after the truth about her upbringing had been revealed in *Cries Unheard* and *The Case of Mary Bell*, the *Daily Mail* featured an interview with Martin Brown's mother. The article still shows a belief in the myth and, using Mrs Richardson's (as she is now) understandable grief and anger as collateral for their viewpoint, they rail at the fact that Mary and Mary's daughter (born by a twist of fate on the anniversary of Martin's death) have anonymity; that she is able to 'lead a normal life'. It mentions the Sereny book, but glosses over the meat of it, stating simply that it gives a 'sympathetic' view of the case and that Mary was paid £50,000 for her contribution to it.* Once a devil has been created in the public imagination, there are those who are ever reluctant to endow the facts with the benefit of any understanding: certainly not with charity, let alone sympathy.

At Seaham, while she was still on remand, Mary got into a fight with another girl who had called her a prostitute. The telling thing about the incident was not that Mary reacted as she did, but that she was terrified that the authorities would want to know how she knew what a prostitute was. That this should genuinely

---

* Ms Sereny is at pains to point out that Mary intended to use the money for her daughter and not for herself. She discusses, at some length, the morality of paying Mary, acknowledging that it raised difficult questions but eventually being satisfied that Mary was not, as the *Daily Mail* suggested, 'profiteering' from her crime.

frighten her – where being accused of murder apparently did not – shows just how much her awareness had been warped by her early experiences. Maybe a form of this irrationality is there in all children: developing brains are apt to choose their own version of what is essential for their self-esteem and ignore other, more important things they find impossible to grasp. Mary was an emotionally disturbed child – of that there is no doubt – but maybe her reactions (or rather, her lack of them) were indicative of the fact that at no time during the whole dreadful business did she really comprehend the dreadful nature of what she had done.

Norma Bell was found not guilty on all counts. Mary Bell was found not guilty of murder, but guilty of the manslaughter of both boys because of diminished responsibility. It was thought, no doubt correctly, that she was a danger to other children. In his judgement, Mr Justice Cusack said:

> If this had been the case of an adult, having regard to the evidence put before me, which I fully accept, that this is a child who is dangerous, I should have felt obliged to impose a life sentence for the reason that, not only did the gravity of the offences warrant it, but that there was evidence of mental disease or abnormality which made it impossible to determine the date when the person concerned could be safely released.
>
> It is an appalling thing that, in a child as young as this, one has to determine such a matter, but I am entirely satisfied that, anxious as I am to do everything for her benefit, my primary duty is to protect other people for the reasons that I have indicated.
>
> I take the view that there is a very grave risk to other children if in fact she is not closely watched and

*every conceivable step taken to see that she does not do
again what it has been found that she did do.*[19]

He sentenced Mary to Detention for Life.

The British justice system agonised over what to do
with the infamous young killer who was now their
responsibility. There was no official precedent, and no
decision they made was going to be a hundred per cent
suitable. The reasons why she had killed two small boys
had not been examined during her trial (they would not
be revealed for years afterwards; as has been said, Mary
herself was not capable of explaining at that time). The
options, loosely speaking, were twofold: in the early
1970s, public opinion was divided (much as it continues to be today) between the reforming approach and
the punitive one.

Mary was to taste both, the latter undoing much of the
good the former had done her. Her years of incarceration
began with hasty short-term measures before she was sent
to the Special Unit of the Red Bank Approved School.
Here she was to find some degree of comfort, warmth and
love. The other detainees were boys. Only five other girls
were sent there during Mary's time, none of them for very
long. Mary grew to dote upon James Dixon, an ex-Navy
man, who ran the school. Five years later, she was sent to
prison until her release in 1980 at the age of 23. She lives
with her partner and her daughter under a new identity.
The injunction that prevents her daughter's identity being
revealed was made permanent on the girl's eighteenth
birthday when it came up for review.

This tragic tale can have no happy ending. Those who
grieve for little Brian and Martin will do so for the rest
of their lives, but the woman who was Mary Bell is not
dangerous, is not evil, and is a good and caring mother

to her daughter. The image of the heartless 'child killer' is still aired whenever possible and those who hope to see beyond it are often viewed with cynicism and suspicion. It's an image that offers some kind of reassurance (we need to *know* who are the bad, and who are the good), and deconstructing it is something we find dangerous and disturbing. To show sympathy to *all* parties in cases like that of Mary Bell, or to attempt to understand how a small child could do such terrible things, is condemned as an act of treachery against the victims. The cynical phrase 'the bleeding heart brigade' suggests a class of people who have been hoodwinked by special pleading, and/or the crocodile tears of a manipulative, wicked sham. It would be easier if this were the case: if the Mary Bell of the tabloids were real and we could recognise evil so easily, society would be better able to eradicate it.

I was chastened, when writing this chapter, by my own reactions to reading about Betty Bell. Having learned about the horrors of Mary's early life and no longer able to believe in the child monster, I found that her mother was the most 'convenient' person to cast as the irredeemable villain. Along with other, more welcome members of the family, Betty turned up regularly at the Red Bank Secure Unit and was a continued presence in Mary's life until her death in 1994. The conflicts that had always existed between the two drew them together in a never-ending tussle of love admixed with hatred. Betty Bell was in many ways a cruel, manipulative and selfish woman and it is easy to revile her. However, her reprehensible and often disgusting behaviour must also have had its root in some horrible trauma. To understand her daughter's history is not enough. Abusers are created by abuse. This is an acknowledged fact, and one that is often disregarded.

Early in 1970, during Mary's time at Red Bank, Gitta Sereny received an anonymous letter together with the following poem, which, the letter said, Mary had written:

'MAM'
I know that in my heart
From you once was not apart
My love for you grows
More each day.
When you visit me mam
Id weep once, your away
I look into your, eyes. So Blue and
theyre very sad, you try to be very
cheery But I know you think Im Bad so Bad
though I really dont know. If you
feel the same,
and treat it as a silly game.
A child who has made criminal fame
Please mam put my tiny mind at ease
Tell Judge and Jury on your knees
They will LISTEN to your cry of PLEAS
THE GUILTY ONE IS you not me.
I sorry IT HAS TO BE this way
Well both cry and you will go away
to other gates were you are free
locked up in prison cells,
Your famley are wee.
these last words I speak, on behalf
of dad, P . . . [Mary's brother] and me
tell them you are guilty
Please, so then mam, Ill be free, Daughter
        May[20]

Mary hadn't, in fact, written the poem at all: Betty had.

5. THE KILLING OF JAMES BULGER

The dust of three decades had settled over the image of the child-turned-killer Mary Bell. A generation had reached adulthood without knowing much about her, or what she'd done; merely that it was dreadful and she was 'evil'. Every so often, the case was given a fresh airing in the tabloids. There was – and still is – 'mileage' in stories about her fight (won in 2002) to preserve her anonymity and that of her daughter. Then, in 1993, another terrible murder rocked the country. The fact that two ten-year-old boys were charged with the crime brought back the same revulsion, the same outrage and the same incredulity that had erupted all those years ago. Once again we looked for the canker in our midst that had turned two innocent-looking children into two particularly repulsive murderers. If, behind those youthful faces, there could be something so vile, so utterly inhuman as to drive them to torture and murder, something or someone had to accept the blame for it: this might be parents; upbringing; the casual acceptance within society of violent images; the widespread breakdown of 'normal' family life; or the decline of Christianity. Generally, it was the easiest option that prevailed. Although all or some of the above factors may have been significant, the truth seemed to be that there was something inherently bad about Robert Thompson and Jon Venables, who had murdered – for no apparent reason and in a most brutal way – a toddler by the name of James Bulger.

Jon Venables was the middle child of three. His brother, three years his senior, and his sister, twelve months his junior, had learning difficulties, but Jon was educationally quite normal. He was born in 1982 to Susan and Neil Venables, in Liverpool. Liverpudlians would not thank anyone for pointing out that they have, on the one hand, a widely perceived image of stoical, open-hearted good humour in the face of unemployment and hardship and are, on the other hand, saddled with the equally famous stereotype of the 'scally': the light-fingered petty thief who survives on what he can 'rob' (as the locals say) or 'fiddle' from the State. Neither of these generalisations can be completely true or (in some cases) completely false: Liverpool has been through a hard time and, though it has a heart, it shows itself also as rough and tough. Children – particularly boys – who grow up in its poorer areas learn how to be streetwise: if you're not 'hard', you suffer the consequences.

Though Jon's parents loved their children and each other, there were problems at home. Neil Venables believed in the kind of old-fashioned relationship his own parents had had, where their roles had been clearly defined by tradition: the man went 'out to work' and provided the money, while the woman stayed home and 'looked after the kids'. In the Venables' case, this division of responsibility was more than usually weighted in the father's favour.

Jon's elder brother, little Paul, was given to temper tantrums. Apart from his learning difficulties, he had a cleft lip: a disability that left him unable to express himself. He was a miserable child, whose constant crying became a real strain on his young mother. When Neil arrived home, her frustrations boiled over and she nagged and complained, but he didn't want to know: it was her job to attend to domestic things and she should just get on with it. Despite this, she adored her children. Jon himself was a smiling, apparently contented baby. He could walk when he was just under a year old; he could speak at fifteen months and was potty-trained early. When his sister, Sandra, came along in 1983, he was happy about the new arrival and protective of her. She was later diagnosed as having problems similar to Paul's but she didn't seem to be frustrated by them in the same way. Both Jon's siblings attended a special school – Meadowbanks – and both seemed to settle down at this school. Jon, meanwhile, was sent to an ordinary primary school. He seemed to be perfectly all right there; the worrying signs didn't surface until he was seven.

In the event, Neil and Susan's marriage didn't carry on along altogether traditional lines, but the two parents managed to find a way of living together that suited them and kept the family together.

In 1983, Susan's father died from cancer and, with her mum now living alone and Susan being aware of her own desperate need for help and adult company, she moved with the kids to their grandmother's house. Neil found a bed-sitting room and continued to visit regularly. He was still sleeping with his wife all this time and he continued to do so even after their divorce. It was a case of keeping the family together, but in two houses rather than one. Journalists would later be suspicious of this arrangement, leaping to the not unreasonable conclusion that it was really a convenient cover for fraudulent benefit claims. Neil had lost his job by this time and money must have been tight, but the couple categorically denied that their domestic arrangements were legally suspect. They had been forced, by their other difficulties, to find a way of making things work for themselves and their young family and living apart was, they thought, the best arrangement.

If this was damaging to any of the children, its effects were not evident. Jon was still a happy child and his brother and sister were adjusting well. The first signs of trouble came when they all moved into a larger house some distance away. Neighbourhood children – children delight in such cruelties – would shout after Jon and call him names because his brother and sister were 'backward'.

His mother reacted to this in much the same way as many parents do: she told him to ignore the taunts and said that 'names would never hurt him'. It's a rather hackneyed phrase and one that is clearly untrue, especially to a child who is suffering because of verbal bullying. Jon may well have also been bullied at his new school; certainly he was showing signs of severe distress and was growing into a problematic child who no one in authority knew how to deal with.

Just after the Christmas recess in 1991, his class teacher at Broad Square Primary noted that he was acting in a worryingly bizarre way. He would sit at his desk, rocking himself to and fro, moaning and making other strange noises. She tried moving him to a seat by her side where she would be able to reassure him, but he wouldn't be pacified. He would knock objects off her desk and fidget throughout the lesson. She later caught him banging his head, hard enough to be causing him pain.

Jon said he was being victimised by the other children. He was often in tears and his work began to suffer. He refused to do as he was told and, though actually capable of much better grades, he was classed as a low achiever. The school staff asked his mother to come and see them with a view to discussing her son's problems. She told them that she, too, was having difficulty with him: he had been abusive to her. She also told them that Jon wanted to be with his brother and sister at their special school. This bears out Gitta Sereny's suggestion that his rocking was an imitation of his brother. He may well have been behaving as he'd seen Paul behave, in an attempt to escape the misery and isolation of his present situation. At the 'special' school, his siblings weren't bullied for being different from normal children: their problems were understood and they were shown care and attention rather than spite.

Nobody knew how to deal with his behaviour and, though it was alarming, he wasn't alone in being problematic and disruptive. However, when a school trip was organised, it was thought that it would be better if he didn't go on it. Even when a social worker (who worked with Jon's brother and sister) offered to accompany him and accept responsibility for him, permission was refused. (Although this is the version of events that the school has put out, Susan Venables maintained that it wasn't true. She had removed him from the trip herself, she claimed, and had asked for her money back.)

Jon's behaviour grew steadily worse. He would roll himself along the walls of the classroom, pulling down pictures and displays in the process. His teacher told how he lay between the desks where he couldn't be reached and refused to emerge. He would cut himself with scissors. Other reported episodes do not seem quite as alarming, but they were adding up to a dangerous level: he covered his face with sticky paper, hung upside down from the coat pegs like a bat and cut holes in his socks. (His mother denied much of this as well. Significantly, she told Gitta Sereny, she never saw any cuts on him and the school had not told her about any of these incidents.)* He took to throwing anything that came to hand across the room. When he was ordered to stand outside the classroom because he'd been naughty, he started hurling things down the corridor. Other parents began to complain that he was creating difficulties for their own children.

One day he tried to strangle another pupil. He came up behind the child and, holding a ruler against the boy's throat, deliberately choked him. It took two teachers to pull Jon away. With hindsight, it's tempting to read a lot into this incident, but it would be unfair to blame his teachers or his parents for not doing so at the time. Children *are* violent – especially boys – and in the rough and tumble of school relationships, they may have assumed Jon had been provoked. However, the violent act could not be ignored. It was decided that a two-day suspension would be an appropriate way to emphasise the seriousness of what he had done. His mother kept him away from school for the next ten weeks. When he came back to formal education, in June 1991, he was put in the same class as Robert Thompson.

Robert's background was, to say the least, tragic. He was one of seven children. In 1971 his mother, Ann, married his father (also called Robert) when they were both eighteen. For her, the marriage may have been – at least subconsciously – an escape from the terrible beatings

---

* In an appendix to *The Case of Mary Bell*.

she regularly suffered at the hands of her drunken father. Her childhood was a catalogue of brutality, both emotional and physical, made even worse by the fact that her elder sister and younger brother escaped most of it: she was the scapegoat. When she told her father that she was getting married, he assumed she was pregnant and, as usual, took his belt to her. He predicted that the union would last twelve months, at most. In fact, it lasted for seventeen years, though there are reports of it being a volatile relationship and of Ann continuing to suffer frequent, sickeningly violent attacks. Whatever the truth, it seems that her husband eventually built up a resentment towards her for, in the end, he started an affair with a woman eighteen years his senior whom he'd met during a family holiday. He didn't attempt to hide his extra-marital activity; on the contrary, he told Ann that if she complained, he would leave his family there and then. There was a furious row, witnessed by the distressed children.

During the seven weeks following that holiday, there was a terrible atmosphere in the Thompson house. Robert would not speak to his wife or sons and spent most of his time either at work or in the pub. Finally, his new partner found them a place to live and he immediately moved in with her, leaving Ann a five-pound note – which was all he was to contribute to his children's upbringing from then on (another version of the story has it that he walked out leaving debts for electricity and gas amounting to £1,500. Ann had only five pounds and was forced to get a crisis loan from the Social Security). They were never to meet 'Big Bobby' again, apart from seeing him across the grave at his mother's funeral. On that occasion he neither spoke to his sons nor even looked at them. Robert was six.

For a boy in his formative years, the huge emotional wrench of losing a father is devastating. In most cases, it is ameliorated by the careful reassurance of both parents: 'Dad still loves you but is going to be living somewhere else'. Without this, the pain will begin to fester.

In October 1988, just seven weeks after 'Big Bobby' had left them, the family returned home from a visit to the boy's grandparents to find their house burned down. They moved into a hostel in Toxteth for two months – a long time for small children and even longer when their lives are in such turmoil. The second eldest boy hated life in the hostel and went to stay with his grandmother. In January the following year they were eventually rehoused in a terrace house, 223 Walton Village.

Ann could no longer cope with her desperate life. She took to drinking extremely heavily, spending her days in a stupor, and keeping a bottle of gin under her pillow to fortify herself as soon as she opened her eyes. The boys were more or less left to fend for themselves. They became known troublemakers and were visited by a succession of social workers. Ann resented these intrusions, in addition to finding them unhelpful and being certain that the social workers were completely unable to understand her plight.

Soon the family began to disintegrate even more. A pattern of bullying developed, going downwards from the older boys to the younger ones, each picking on the next. The boys began 'sagging' (playing truant), some because they wanted to, others because their older siblings threatened them with a kicking if they didn't. The younger ones suffered because of the reputation their name carried and, as they grew, they learned to cope by living up to their notoriety. The family had become infamous and the vicious circle was on a fast downward spiral. One of the older boys accused his brother of chaining him up in the pigeon shed and 'tarring and feathering' him. It was denied of course and charges were eventually dropped, but witnesses say that it did happen. Soon afterwards, the brother who'd been arrested for the alleged assault found himself in trouble again, this time for stealing a motorcycle.

Young Robert's immediate senior was, by now, out of control, sniffing aerosol fumes and experimenting with other drugs. He had a history of police cautions for minor offences. He once took Robert with him on a 'job', where he was caught stealing several thousand pounds' worth of computer equipment from a solicitor's office. Ann, quite unable to do anything with him and getting frantic, burned all his clothes except for his school uniform. It was intended to keep him at home, but it didn't work. He went into voluntary care after he pulled a knife on one of his brothers.

Ann met another 'Bob' and gave birth to yet another son (she'd always wanted a daughter) in May 1992. For a while, during her pregnancy and immediately after-wards, things settled down: she stopped drinking and felt happier. Then, during a row, she again took a swipe at one of her children (the eldest still with her: one who'd done his best to keep the family together). He contacted the social services and told them he wanted to be taken away from home. Both Thompson boys in local authority care were, later, to overdose on pills, yet their mother remembers their leaving as an amicable arrangement in each case, which resulted in happier, more stable lives for both of them.

Meanwhile, during his truanting jaunts, Robert was 'robbing' from the local shops. Neighbours remember him as a 'tearaway' but not a bad lad. His brother maintained that he (Robert) was 'frightened of his own shadow . . . sometimes he tries to act big'.[1] Unknown to any of them, maybe even to himself, young Robert Thompson was in turmoil.

In June 1991, Jon Venables was transferred to St Mary's Church of England Primary School in Walton. Robert Thompson had been attending the same school since 1989 but, like Jon, he was placed in a class one year below his age group in an attempt to match the work to his existing capabilities. Here, Jon and Robert struck up a friendship, though Jon later said that he avoided Robert in school because he was 'trouble'. He was more than happy, though, to imitate Robert's bad habits, and soon the two of them were off 'sagging' and 'robbing' together. Their teacher at this time (a man with particular skills in the handling of disturbed children) was beginning to make something of a difference with Jon even though the boy still misbehaved when outside the classroom. The strange head-banging and moaning were still occurring; he reacted badly to any kind of rebuke and he and his new friend were getting into fights.

The image of the two of them together (an image perpetuated by the newspapers after the murder of James Bulger) is of the reprobate, Robert – aggressive, headstrong and thuggish – with his quieter, impressionable side-kick tagging along, doing whatever Robert suggests. This is too simple a view but it's easy to see how it came about. Robert was the more hard-faced: he lied easily – even when presented with indisputable evidence – and he cried on cue. However, according to his teacher he was easier to handle in the classroom than

Jon. Jon would accept discipline for a short time and then go back to causing trouble later. He had a short temper, was much more of a handful in class than Robert and was 'disruptive and lazy'.

Robert was a bully: he forced his younger brother to play truant. The boy told his teacher that Robert had threatened to break his glasses if he refused. It was the same sort of treatment Robert himself had received from his older siblings: he was responding to the lessons he had been taught. Both boys were a volatile mixture of pain, anger and fear but, on the face of it, they were simply badly behaved and, compared with their young colleagues, not remarkably so at that.

In September 1992, the two boys moved into a different class, away from the calming influence of their previous teacher. From a casual glance it might appear that both were truanting together for most of the time. In the autumn term of 1992, Robert was missing from school for 49 half-days and Jon 50, both out of a possible 140 half-days. However, there were only 5 half-days when they were absent together and 35 of Jon's absences were because of an operation to correct a squint in his eye. On the first day of that term, Mr and Mrs Venables caught him wandering the streets and took him back to school.

These two severely unhappy little boys had been separated in the classroom. In November 1992, after one of their truanting episodes, it was decided to keep them completely apart: in different classes, in fact. They were kept in at playtime and were supervised separately – indoors – at lunchtime.

They were in trouble and they knew it. When pressed about what they did when not on school premises, they both admitted to stealing but each blamed the other for it. This is exactly what one might expect children to do but, not long afterwards, there were to be far more serious implications when they did exactly the same thing on being asked which of them had instigated the murder of James Bulger.

The parents of both boys were asked to come into school. Susan Venables shouted at her son; Ann Thompson showed her desperation when she told Robert's teacher that Robert had run away from home and, when he'd eventually returned, she'd hidden his shoes to prevent any repetition. She later took Robert to the local police station and asked an officer to have a word with him about his behaviour. She told him he would end up in the cells if he were not careful.

There was a different side to Robert: he was a caring, vulnerable son, who collected 'trolls' (most of which he had stolen) and who sucked his thumb. He was good with the baby and helped his mother to bake. He would sometimes sit on her lap and play with her ear. He had friends, including a 'girlfriend' who lived across the road. She had a younger brother, whom Robert would defend against older boys who picked on him.

During the spring of 1993, Robert's little brother was found wandering around the Strand Shopping Precinct in Bootle. He was upset and crying and when asked what had happened, he said that Robert and another boy (it wasn't Jon) had taken him there and left him. He said that Robert had hit him and kicked him and then disappeared, leaving him to find his own way home.

At the end of January shoppers might have noticed two boys hanging around in the Strand, trying to attract the attention of a toddler. One was tapping on the window of a shop and beckoning to the child to come outside. The child didn't want to and after showing some initial interest he turned back to his mother's side. The boys disappeared, but their behaviour had been seen and noted. Some time later, the man who had observed them was able to identify Jon Venables.

They had fantasised about committing a murder before. They once asked a local boy if he wanted to be in their gang: 'We're going to kill someone.'[2] This could, of course, be interpreted in all sorts of ways: as a game; a make-believe adventure, no more dangerous than the 'bang bang, you're dead!' games that most boys play. Alternatively, they might have meant to 'kill' in the sense of 'beat up' – many children have used the word in that way and though it's unpleasant enough, Robert and Jon might not have meant it literally – at least not at that point.

The atmosphere in James Bulger's home was very different from that of both the Thompson and Venables households. Both his parents, Ralph and Denise, came from very large families (Denise's mother had had three children by one father. She was widowed during the latter part of WW2, later remarried and then had ten more children, of whom Denise was the second youngest. Ralph was one of six brothers and sisters).

Ralph and Denise lived close to each other and were supportive and loving. Their lives were difficult at times, but they got on with things and took strength from those around them. This was particularly needed when the couple's first child, a daughter, was stillborn. They decided to marry soon afterwards and tied the knot in September 1989 on Denise's 22nd birthday.

James Patrick was born on 16 March 1990. He was named after his late paternal grandfather. His uncle (Ralph's brother) was also called James Patrick. The new arrival later proved to be a bubbly, spirited child, who revelled in the attention of the many adults around him and in the fun and games he enjoyed with his female cousins. Denise remembers him imitating Michael Jackson's dancing and playing videotapes of the pop star over and over again. He liked books and, helped by his parents and other relatives, was reading at an early age.

To look back on this happy child in the light of what we now know was to befall him is heartbreaking. His favourite toys; the special armchair that his dad had made for him; his delight at seeing the police helicopter fly over the house; the smart clothes he wore at Christmas: all have a terrible poignancy. Those memories and the lasting grief belong with his family alone and it would be crass to say that we, who did not know the little boy, feel even a particle of the sorrow they share. However, if we are to look at the cruel and wicked murder of James by Robert Thompson and Jon Venables, we must remember that it happened at the very point where he was emerging as a person. His baby years were nearly over and he was developing a personality that was trusting and warm. His nature was a reflection of the love that surrounded him, just as the two boys who killed him reflected their own backgrounds.

It was Friday 12 February 1993, the last day before the half-term holiday, and Jon had asked his mother if he could bring the class gerbils home, in order to care for them during the break. She had told him, yes, he could, and he was looking forward to it. He wasn't a regular truant and the gerbils gave him reason enough to want to be in school that day, but in the event, he didn't make it. Perhaps he and Robert had already decided to 'sag'. His teacher remembered that Jon had been particularly badly behaved the day before: more than she'd ever known him to be. He had seemed to be excited about something.

On that final day of school he met Robert and they decided to truant. Robert was with his younger brother who didn't want to go with them. The brother was looking forward to the pottery class. Perhaps fortunately for him, Robert allowed him to leave and make his own way to school. Robert and Jon were seen 'sagging off' by one of their classmates, who reported them to their teacher. The headmistress rang the Education Welfare Officer and tried to call Susan Venables, but she wasn't at home.

The two boys went, as they often did, to the Strand shopping centre in Bootle. It was a good place to hang around on a cold day and there were plenty of opportunities to indulge in one of their favourite pastimes, 'robbing' from the shops. They were challenged, first in a card shop, where they were planning to 'rob' some trolls for Robert's collection. They told the woman behind the counter that they were off school for half term and that they were with their mum. She was probably relieved when they ran out of the shop: now they were going to be somebody else's problem.

Any account of that day will inevitably be punctuated with the agonising phrase: 'if only'. 'If only' that woman had detained them – she didn't, but not many people would see badly behaved boys as their responsibility: in a place like Liverpool there are simply too many of them. Throughout that Friday, two ten-year-olds, obvious truants and clearly up to no good, wandered around unchecked. There is no blame to apportion here: what could anybody have done? If an adult had tried to apprehend them, it may well have aroused suspicions about his or her motive. The most common response to troublesome children is to avoid getting involved and to hope for the best. The few people who do take it upon themselves to intervene are frequently seen as cranks, busybodies, or even worse. Later, when James was seen accompanying the pair, there might well have been sufficient cause for intervention. However, even then no one could have ever suspected what was happening in front of them.

Robert stole a clockwork soldier and tried to make it crawl up the handrail of the escalator. It fell off, of course, but they weren't too bothered: the fun was in the taking, not in the having. A woman scolded them: the toy could have jammed the mechanism. They ignored her. The same woman saw them some time later: she witnessed their first attempt to abduct a child.

It was getting on for half past twelve, outside the department store TJ Hughes. A mother, out with her son and daughter, noticed the two schoolboys and wondered what they were up to. Her children, still toddlers, wandered up to one of the pair, who was kneeling down to the their level and encouraging them by opening purses on the lower shelf of a display stand and snapping them shut. The boy turned to his friend and said, 'Shall we take one of these?'[3] The woman assumed they were referring to something they wanted to steal, but they may well have been deciding which of her children they were going to take. She called her children back to her and went to the till in order to pay for the goods she'd selected. Her son continued to find the boys' behaviour intriguing, and he was tempted over to them three times. On each occasion, the mother had to call him back. Having paid for her shopping, she turned round to find he was missing yet again. Sure enough, her little girl said he'd 'gone outside with the boys.'[4] She panicked and, grabbing her daughter by the hand, rushed back to where she'd seen the two attracting her children's attention. They were not there. She was lucky; very lucky indeed. She glanced in a certain direction and was just able to catch sight of her boy as he disappeared behind some benches. Robert and Jon were luring him on by playing 'chase': running a little way and then stopping to allow him to catch up. One of them went behind a pillar and, teasing him by half-hiding, beckoned him still further. The anxious mother shouted, but he wasn't listening; he was too engrossed in the game.

As soon as he realised that an adult had seen them, Robert or Jon – whichever one of them was beckoning – stopped and told the boy, 'Go back to your mum.'[5] He seemed quite relaxed about the whole thing and was smiling at the mother. She considered reporting the incident, but decided that it would probably be more trouble than it was worth. Her son was safe: that was the main thing. Had she not caught sight of him in that split second, we might never have heard the name of James Bulger and a different family would have had to endure the horror of that day.

On this particular Friday Denise Bulger was going, as she normally did, to her mother's house. Her mother wasn't in but, as usual, there were other members of the family coming and going. James played with his young cousin, Antonia. It seemed to be the beginning of a typical day.

Her brother's fiancée Nicola, who was minding their niece (brother John's girl, Vanessa), popped her head round the door. She was going into Bootle to return some underwear, which had turned out to be the wrong size. Denise, knowing how much James enjoyed a ride in a car, readily agreed to accompany her. She was a protective mother and, knowing James to be adventurous, would normally have taken him out in his pram where she could keep an eye on him. This time, it wouldn't be worth the trouble: they weren't going to be out for very long. They arrived at the Strand precinct at half past two.

James wore his blue hooded anorak, grey tracksuit and 'Noddy' T-shirt. He also had on a blue scarf with yellow stripes, with a picture of a cat on it. His blond hair and cherubic face made him look like a doll. Pictures of him show him to have been a truly beautiful child, with a happy, smiling face.

He was enjoying the freedom to walk around for once and played running games with his cousin while Nicola sorted out her purchase. The group then went to buy something to eat, after which they visited Marks & Spencer's to buy some groceries. James kept running around and, on more than one occasion, Denise had to tell him to stay close to her. After a trip to Tesco the kids were becoming restive. James was complaining about having to hold his mother's hand. Nicola bought some sweets; James tried to go on the escalator, but Denise told him he mustn't. He complained loudly about this, attracting the attention of a passer-by who (it's a bitter irony that she did) asked what was the matter with the child.

They were ready to go home now. Denise said she wanted to go to the butcher's to buy something for their 'tea'. They trooped off to AR Tyms' where Nicola queued for some cooked meat and Denise went to buy some chops. James was by her side.

She had the exact money ready and ought, really, to have been in and out of the shop in short order, but the assistant mistook her instructions and didn't give her the meat that she had pointed out. James wandered about the shop a little and then stood in the doorway.

And then it happened: Denise handed over the money, but when she turned round, James was no longer there. She asked Vanessa where he'd gone. Vanessa said she wasn't sure but, when asked again, she told her aunt that James had gone off into the precinct. Denise felt a surge of panic.

She ran out of the shop and looked around anxiously. The Strand was crowded with shoppers and James was nowhere to be seen. Nicola joined her and the two women, with the little girl in tow, went off in a desperate search.

It had been a second or two – no more – during which James had done exactly what the other little boy had done earlier that day. As his mother and aunt raced towards the security office, he was already toddling off, holding on to Jon Venables' hand. This moment of time, recorded as it was on CCTV screens, has since become infamous: the trusting baby with two small boys. That sequence, more than any words, captures the dreadful impotence of hindsight: 'if only' somebody had stopped them; 'if only' Denise had seen him leaving her side; 'if only . . .'

It may never be known whether Robert Thompson and Jon Venables took James with the specific intention of murdering him. There are many theories as to why they did what they did. In his book, *Destroying the Baby in Themselves*, David Jackson puts forward the theory that they may have been trying to eradicate that aspect of themselves that they saw as less than masculine. Alternatively, they may have seen James as a substitute for their younger siblings and, in a perverted way, may have been seeking revenge (Robert told the police that if he had wanted to murder a baby, he would have murdered his own). The murder may even have been sexually motivated – a way of asserting power, which they felt they lacked. Their violence could have escalated in a natural progression: spitefulness, then nasty bullying, which then became more and more vicious. It may, dreadfully, have been a way of ridding themselves of a little boy with whom they'd had their fun and with whom they no longer wanted to be burdened.

At 3.43, the group were recorded leaving the Strand by the Marks & Spencer's exit. They walked up Stanley Road, with James by now crying for his mother. They shouted at him, 'Are you all right? You were told not to run!'[6] Jon held the little boy's hand and they went on their way, ignoring his distress. There were times when he seemed to forget his tears and was seen running along quite happily. To any of the 38 people who witnessed the three together, nothing seemed in the least suspicious.

They went down to the canal where (according to Jon's statement) Robert suggested they throw James into the water. James wouldn't do what they wanted, which was to kneel down to look at his reflection. Unable to dupe him into going near the edge, one or the other of the pair picked him up and dropped him, cutting his head. He kept saying 'I want my mummy.'[7]

They left him there, crying by the side of the canal. A woman saw him, but thought that he must be with other children who were close by. Robert and Jon came back for him: 'Come on, baby,' they said. With his forehead bruised and cut, he followed them, expecting them to look after him as all the older children he knew had always done. The pair didn't want his injuries to be seen, so they covered his forehead with his hood. They crossed the road, witnessed by passers-by who remembered his tear-stained face. This was not an unusual scene; nobody saw it as suspicious.

They continued walking the little boy around the town. They climbed over walls and walked past busy shops – all in full view. No one challenged them and James wasn't able to tell anyone that he ought not to have been with these two boys. At times they became impatient with him. A motorist saw them pulling him on as he resisted them, obviously not wanting to go further. Robert kicked him lightly in the ribs to get him moving. The driver described it as a 'persuasion kick'.[8]

The afternoon was drawing to a close. The evening rush hour had started and the three were seen by many people: they seemed to be three brothers, the two older ones having to look after a reluctant younger boy. A woman on a bus saw them swinging James in the air, each holding one of his hands. She thought they were being too rough with him and said as much to her daughter.

What was once a reservoir at Breeze Hill had been filled in and grassed over. It was there they sat and rested for a while. A woman, who was drawing her curtains against the approach of darkness, saw Jon shake James violently.

Another woman, out with her dog, came across the group and asked why James was crying. She was told by the two older boys that they had found him and that they were going to take him to the local police station. She noticed his injured head and told them to be sure they did. They walked off in a different direction to the police station, and she called after them. She was worried about the child and might have gone after them had somebody else not come along just then and told her that she had seen the little boy laughing not long before and that he had seemed to be all right.

They walked along a busy high street, where they went into a DIY shop and asked where the nearest sweet shop was. The man they spoke to noted the little boy's evident distress. They next went into a pet shop, where they gazed at the fish. At this time, they may already have decided on James's fate, or they may simply have been meandering, looking for something to do. James was quieter by now. He was probably extremely tired, having been marched around for over an hour. His head must have been hurting and, now the reassuring daylight had gone, the safety of home and the presence of his mum and dad must have seemed worlds away.

They carried on walking and, some time later, met a twelve-year-old boy who knew Robert. He could see James's bruises; could tell that he was not happy and had, in fact, been crying. When asked what had happened, the two said that James had fallen and invited the boy to look more closely at another bruise under James's hair. They made out that he was Jon's brother and that they were taking him home. The boy said that they better had, or he would 'batter' them.

In City Road, they detached James's hood from his coat and threw it into a tree. Soon afterwards, they met a man who also knew Robert and who saw that James was sobbing. Robert had climbed on top of a wall and it was Jon who told the man, 'I'm fed up of having my little brother. He's always the same.' He added, 'I'm not bringing him again.'[9]

The last person to see them was a fourteen-year-old girl and her father. They were not far from Walton Lane Police Station, on a busy road. The girl saw them pushing James out into the traffic and, as she thought at the time, the little boy was laughing. They realised she'd seen them and, before the adult could intervene, they quickly took James through a gap in a fence, which led to the railway.

When they came away from the railway line, James was no longer with them. They continued to mooch around and no one who met them would see the slightest peculiarity in their behaviour. They went to the house of a friend of theirs but he wasn't in. They stayed for a little while in front of his house and then went off to visit a local video shop. Susan Venables found them there and 'collared' her son. She had been looking for him everywhere and was furious with him. She pulled the two boys out of the shop, allowing Robert to run off. Determined to have Jon see the error of his ways, Susan hauled him off to the police station and asked the officer to give him a 'talking to'. Later, she explained to him why she'd been so angry: a little boy had gone missing from the Strand Shopping Centre. Whoever had taken him was still on the loose – did Jon want to end up as his next victim?

Robert, meanwhile, had run home to his mother and complained to her that Susan had thrown him out of the video store. Ann was outraged about this and took Robert to the police station to report the incident. In *Every Mother's Nightmare* Mark Thomas points out the anomaly: both killers were taken to the local police station within a few hours of having committed a murder.

* * *

The story of the missing toddler was all over the news. The Bulger family were frantic, but were holding on to any shred of hope. In a cruelly deceptive way the CCTV images were encouraging. Denise thought that if James had been taken by two young boys, then the most likely outcome was that they were hanging about somewhere playing, and would eventually get bored with him and let him go. A known sex offender had been in the Strand that day, but the police had questioned him and were satisfied that he knew nothing about James's disappearance. As the next few agonising days passed, the whole country was gripped by the events in Liverpool. The grainy picture of Robert and Jon leading James to his fate was haunting the TV screens and everyone hoped, everyone thought, that there would be a happy ending.

Four boys found James on the Sunday afternoon. The body was in such a mess that at first they didn't know what they were looking at: it might have been a smashed doll. He had been laid across the railway track and a train had cut his little body in two. The top half, which looked at first like a bundle of discarded clothes, was a shocking sight: his hair was matted with blood and he was a mass of 42 cuts and bruises. The lower half was naked and was found further down the line. The boys had thrown blue paint into his eyes; they had hit him with bricks and stones and had battered him with an iron bar. It is possible that they had forced batteries into his rectum. Before leaving him, they had covered his head with bricks, so that the driver of the oncoming train wouldn't see him.

Members of the public started to lay flowers at the spot. Among them was a little boy with an open, pretty face. He had brought a single rose 'for the baby'. His name was Robert Thompson.

The huge outcry that followed spread throughout the country and then abroad. It was known that the police were looking for two boys in connection with the murder and people everywhere were incredulous, scandalised and very angry. The case was seen as evidence of a malign influence that was spreading like cancer through the younger generation and had to be stamped out by any means possible.

A boy, Philip Edwards (not his real name), was arrested after a secret tip-off from his father. Within minutes of the police arriving surreptitiously to take him in for questioning, reporters, photographers and TV cameramen had arrived at his house. A mob of angry people gathered with them. In the regrettable and all too familiar way that these things happen, Philip had been accused, tried and sentenced on a basis of mere suspicion. The officers who questioned him soon knew they were on the wrong track, but this realisation came too late for the Edwards family, who had to move house to escape physical harm. Philip himself – a boy who had never been in any kind of trouble before – began to have nightmares and showed classic signs of severe emotional disturbance. He said that, during the bewildering and frightening time with the police, he had actually persuaded himself that he was responsible for killing James. The reliability of confessions has been called into question many times in the past and this boy's experience provides yet another instance of stress resulting in auto-suggestion.

After this, a formal strategy for dealing with the press was put into operation. Regular briefings were organised and the murder team were able to persuade the journalists that any assumptions that the press might have in future were not going to help catch the killers and would only add to the anguish of the Bulger family.

The police were in no way responsible for the alarming repercussions of that incident, but they were wary of it happening again. When a woman came in with what seemed like a promising lead, they trod very carefully. She knew the Venables; she knew that Jon had been truanting on the day of the murder and that he had come home with blue paint all over his coat. Jon looked like one of the boys on the security video; he had a friend called Robert, who he'd been with and who therefore could well be the second child. Police officers called at the homes of both boys, taking care not to let the neighbours know who they were, or what their business was.

Jon's coat did have blue paint on it: there was a print on the sleeve that could have been where James had grabbed him. His mother, unable to comprehend the enormity of the situation, responded as though the officers were visiting because of Jon's habitual truancy. Jon himself blamed Robert for their presence, complaining: 'It's that Robert Thompson. He always gets me into trouble.'

Robert's immediate response when called on by police was to blurt out: 'I didn't kill him.'[10]

The formal questioning of the two boys was going to be a difficult and harrowing task. They were smaller and younger than the police had supposed from the video and the natural repulsion the officers felt about the crime had to be suppressed if they were to find out the truth of what had happened.

Robert was interviewed by Detective Sergeant Phil Roberts and Detective Constable Bob Jacobs. His mother was present at the time and he was given appropriate legal representation. He behaved much as he did when he was in trouble at school: he denied everything and showed himself to be artful and defensive. He admitted that he hadn't been at school on the day in question and that he'd been with Jon. Significantly, he said that he remembered seeing James and his mother; it was extremely unlikely that he would recall two strangers among so many people, but this proved nothing. He said they'd then left the Strand for the library, after which he'd gone home. Jon, on the other hand, admitted having been with Robert, but said they hadn't been anywhere near the shopping centre – this again could easily have been the understandable lie of a child who simply wanted to demonstrate genuine innocence.

When the detectives asked Robert why he supposed Jon would deny being at the Strand, Robert began to incriminate his friend, but he suggested a watered-down version of their involvement. Perhaps, he said, Jon had done something bad. Perhaps he *had* taken the baby and then lost him. The detectives pointed out that one of the boys in the CCTV picture was wearing a jacket much the same as the one Robert had. He proved equal to this: 'Lots of jackets are sold that are the same as mine,'[11] he said. They persisted. The other boy in the picture, they argued, had a coat that looked like Jon's, and that wasn't such a common design. Robert put the onus back on Jon: 'Yeah, well, he's not walking along with me.' His bluff began to crack as the idea of Jon, rather than himself, being the guilty party grew in his mind. Soon he wasn't merely suggesting that Jon might have been involved; he was stating it:

Detective Roberts: We believe that you left with baby
   James and with Jon.
Robert Thompson: Who says?
Detective Roberts: We say, now.
Robert Thompson: No. I never left with him.
Detective Roberts: Well, tell me what happened, then.
Robert Thompson: It shows in the paper that Jon had
   hold of his hand.[12]

He wept easily, as he had often done: without tears,
stopping his fake sobs abruptly when they had achieved
their effect and the adults had eased up on their more
difficult questions. His story changed slightly, but stuck
to the fundamental idea that Jon had taken James and
that he (Robert) had left the two of them somewhere in
town. The next morning, more of the truth crept in:
both older boys had gone to the railway with James and
he (Robert) had then gone off alone because Jon had
thrown paint in the baby's eyes.

The one thing that seemed to hit home was mention of
the batteries that had been found. Robert went bright red
(he said it was because he was too hot) and refused to
admit any knowledge of them. His brother had once been
accused – and cleared – of the sexual assault of another
boy and it is very likely that Robert himself had suffered
similar abuse. Later, when he was asked why James's
trousers and underwear had been removed, he squirmed
with embarrassment and declared: 'I'm not a pervert, you
know . . . How would you like me calling you a pervert?'
He was getting more and more worked up, protesting to
his mother: 'He said I'm a pervert, they said I've played
with his willy.'[13] The interviewer tried another tack. He
asked what Robert thought Jon would say if they asked
him about the missing clothing, and Robert, fully aware

that Jon would be just as keen to put the whole story the other way round in order to extricate himself, admitted it. Jon would say that he, Robert, had taken the baby's trousers down and played with his privates.

The interviews with Jon were every bit as difficult but, where Robert was defiant and canny, Jon was scared, weepy and, at times, hysterical. Predictably, like Robert, he was quick to portray his friend as the more culpable of the two. Robert was a troublemaker, he said, and he'd often tried to avoid his company. It may be that this was partly true: the Thompsons certainly had a bad reputation and Robert would not have been a mother's favourite choice of friend for her son. Jon also referred to Robert's vulnerable side: that he played with girls, collected 'troll' dolls and sucked his thumb. Boys, like girls, are often subjected to sexist stereotyping. Presented with the notion that 'boys don't cry', they are taught from before puberty that being male means eschewing all signs of sensitivity. Fearing that, alone among their peers, they can never live up to the aggressively tough persona that is required of them, they learn to despise signs of weakness in others lest they themselves be seen as suspect.

As with Robert, the admissions started to filter through. At first, Jon insisted that he 'never' took James. The next day, he admitted that he *had* taken him away from the Strand – but that he had left him in the company of Robert, at the canal. The detectives had a feeling that Jon subconsciously wanted to admit his guilt, but that he was being held back from a full confession because of his parents' presence: particularly his mother, to whom he constantly turned when the questioning became difficult for him. He was, in fact, saying what he knew she wanted to hear. They had a quiet word with her: would she tell her son that, no matter what he'd done, she still loved him? Utterly traumatised and no doubt dreading what was to come, Susan agreed. After persuading Neil to support her, she somehow managed to do as she'd been asked. The hunch had been exactly right. Almost at once, Jon burst into tears and blurted out: 'I did kill him.' He added, 'What about his mum? Will you tell her I'm sorry?'[14]

The rest of the ghastly story poured out, with Robert as the major culprit. It had been Robert's idea to murder James, Jon declared: Robert had wanted to throw him in the canal, but James wouldn't go near the water. Robert had picked him up and hurt him. Yes, he – Jon – had thrown James's hood into the tree. They had gone to the railway and Robert had thrown bricks at James; Jon had only thrown very small stones and none of them at James's head. Robert had thrown the blue paint over him; the bricks had knocked James over; he was screaming, but had managed to get up each time he fell. Robert had told him to stay down; he had hit him with an iron bar. James had fallen onto the railway track and Jon had said: 'Don't you think we've done enough now?' Robert was the one who had taken James's clothes off, although Jon admitted to removing his shoes. Robert had kicked James in the face and in the groin.

Jon wouldn't talk about 'the worst bit'. When asked about the batteries, he went into hysterics. The detectives asked him if Robert had sexually interfered with James, but he wouldn't – or couldn't – respond. He began to hit his father and wept uncontrollably.

They were known throughout the ensuing trial as Child A (Robert) and Child B (Jon). Throughout their interviews with the police, as they were about to stand trial, and during the weeks that the proceedings lasted, the two boys were treated with as much care and concern as was thought appropriate for their age. Naturally, this 'soft' approach found no favour with a large section of the press who, unable to reveal the names of the alleged killers, nevertheless went as far as they could to build up a picture of two juvenile maniacs who were now being pampered at the expense of the taxpayer. In *The Sleep of Reason* David James Smith details the reaction of the *Sun*, which bore a large picture of Jon being led into court. His face was obscured in order to comply with legal requirements, but the picture was intended to provoke indignation: Jon was carrying a lollipop and the policeman who accompanied him had a protective hand on his shoulder. The accompanying pages described, as Mr Smith put it: 'In some selective and spurious detail', the supposed luxury in which the two alleged murderers were kept as they awaited justice. There was a rash of comments from 'hard-line' politicians, generally pandering to the public's paranoia and outrage. This was to be the tone of much, though not all, of the reporting of the case, and was to continue long afterwards.

Given their youth and a desire to determine their culpability in legal terms that would be scrupulously fair to all sides, it was going to be nearly impossible to reach a wholly satisfactory compromise between the gravity of the trial and making sure that the boys were not unfairly intimidated by it. Robert and Jon were brought into the old-fashioned Court Number One at Preston three weeks before the start of the proceedings, so that the surroundings would be less daunting for them. The court would operate from 10.30 to 3.30, to reflect school hours. One disputed concession was the way the boys were seated. This was on a raised platform within the dock, so that they would be able to see what was happening around them. This, it was later contended, could have made them feel over-exposed and therefore vulnerable.

It was deemed advisable to have the free-standing chairs in the public gallery replaced by fixed seats, lest angry spectators be tempted to throw them. Journalists who attended the actual trial, or who listened to it from a nearby office via a radio link, were briefed on what they were allowed to report. They were asked to confirm that they understood and then made to sign documents to this effect. Rigorous security surrounded the court-room: spectators were asked to go through an airport-style metal detector and were then searched with a hand-held device. No chances were taken: public order and the boys' safety was paramount.

As in the trial of Mary and Norma Bell, there was a distinct difference in the attitudes of the defendants. Both boys had gained weight. Robert, his hair cropped close (at his own request), appeared to be completely composed, while Jon had obviously been crying and seemed frightened and overawed. The presence of Jon's parents and the absence of Robert's was also open to interpretation. Erroneous opinions were already being formed.

Denise Bulger was, by this time, in the last stages of pregnancy and therefore was not in court. Ralph Bulger was present and once more impressed many people with his dignity and restraint, as both James's parents did throughout the trial. He was to attend on the Monday and Tuesday, but was with his wife on Wednesday. After the following day's gruelling testimony, he decided not to go back and issued a statement to that effect. In the event, both he and Denise did come back in time for the final stages of Mr Justice Morland's summing-up and for the verdict.

In a shock move, Robert's defence counsel opened by asserting that it would be impossible to give the accused a fair trial because of the huge amount of adverse publicity the case had generated in the press. Jon's counsel seconded this motion but, naturally, the prosecution contested it. That the two had abducted James was not in dispute. The main area for deliberation, the prosecuting counsel said, was going to be Robert's version of events over Jon's. The jury were perfectly capable of ignoring the prejudicial accounts they might have read and would be able to make up their minds from the evidence that was to be put before them. The judge agreed.

After telling the terrible story of James's abduction and murder to the court, the prosecution counsel, on the second day, went into some detail about the boys' taped interviews with the police. Using transcripts, he demonstrated how Robert denied everything at first, but went on to admit to being present. Throughout, Robert had stuck to his contention that it was Jon who had tortured and killed James. He had been astute enough to say that he had lifted James to see whether or not he was still breathing, thereby explaining the presence of blood on his own clothing. Jon was clearly astonished at this. He turned, open-mouthed, towards Robert, but was unable to see him because a social worker was sitting between them. When it came to Jon's tale, it depicted almost an exact reversal of roles: admitting to his presence and some minor acts of violence (he had only thrown small stones and had deliberately missed with many of them), but saying it was Robert who had really been responsible.

The case hinged on which (if either) of the boys was telling the truth, and whether they knew that what they were doing was wrong. Neither boy was asked to go into the witness box, but the recordings of the interviews by detectives were played in full. Each of the two defence barristers, unable to dispute the involvement of their client, put the weight of responsibility on the other boy. No one but Robert and Jon know what actually did happen on that awful day, but it would seem incredible to suppose, as Robert claimed, that he had stood by and watched while Jon murdered James. Jon's account, that he took part half-heartedly, also seems very difficult to believe.

The jury found both guilty and they were detained at Her Majesty's Pleasure. Jon wept openly, while even Robert seemed close to tears for the first time. The order banning the press from using their real names was removed, but a different order replaced it. This was to the effect that information about their subsequent whereabouts should not be open to public scrutiny. The two little boys who had shaken the world were led away to separate secure units. They were never to meet each other again.

Robert Thompson and Jon Venables may be able to repair something of their lives, but they will never be normal people. According to reports, they have come to terms with the evil thing they did. Jon did so much earlier than Robert, who continued to deny it for many years. Ironically, and to many people's bitter criticism, they both received a far better education – moral, emotional and academic – than they would ever have had if they had not committed the crime. The issues surrounding their punishment remain the subject of deep division. Some feel that they have been 'rewarded' for what they did; others believe they have been successfully rehabilitated and steered away from the desperate and dangerous lives that they would otherwise almost certainly have led. It is extremely unlikely that either of them poses the danger to others that they once did. Though there is a strong belief that they should have served time in an adult prison in order that the Bulger family should have even partial justice, there is a weight of opinion that disagrees. Like other children who have killed, Robert and Jon have grown up and, thankfully, they have changed.

They were released in 2001 amid much controversy about whether or not the Home Secretary had the right to impose longer 'tariffs' than had been set by the Trial Judge. Although their whereabouts has always been protected information, tales of their supposed lives of luxury during their years of detention surfaced every so often – whenever the press could get their hands on any juicy morsel, in fact – as well as anything that seemed to confirm that they were (as they had first been described) 'evil'.

Leon McEwan, a seventeen-year-old who was in the same secure unit as Robert between 1998 and 1999, took his story to the *Manchester Evening News*, apparently motivated by press reports of Ralph Bulger's abortive attempts to overturn the decision made by the Lord Chief Justice, Lord Woolf, to reduce both Thompson and Venables' minimum term to seven years and eight months. The teenager said that Robert Thompson 'didn't seem to be sorry for what he'd done'. Furthermore, he had boasted about torturing animals and had flown into a rage when his picture appeared on the television. As if this image of an unstable, unreformed maniac were not enough, McEwan was able to include an inconsequential bit of 'news', the publication of which could only have been intended to provoke further outrage: that Robert had been allowed on days out to the Trafford shopping centre in Manchester, accompanied by members of his family.

Jon Venables was haunted by his crime and told of his dreams of another baby James waiting to be born, growing inside him. Robert Thompson took far longer even to begin to appreciate what he had done and to try to come to terms with it. Because of this, rumours have continued to circulate about his alleged unrepentant, violent nature. Any reasonable discussion about what happened and the reasons behind it has been accompanied by tabloid articles, drenched in lurid, negative adjectives. These culminated in two reported incidents – one fabricated, the other exaggerated out of all proportion. In February 2001, these were cited in a challenge to the Lord Chief Justice, who had ruled that the two boys, then aged eighteen, were eligible for parole.

The first was alleged to have occurred in January 1997 when Robert was fourteen. Reports were published of a fight between him and another boy – a sixteen-year-old inmate who had battered his mother to death with a hammer. According to a leaked official incident report, they had been arguing over 'who had committed the most evil crime'.

In the second incident, another boy, Scott Walker, alleged that Robert had come into his room and attempted to strangle him with a flex. He admitted having taunted Robert previously, but said that any boy who reacted to innocuous jibes by attempting murder was not fit to be set free.

In fact, the 'official incident report', on which the first story had been based, proved to have been forged on a blank form obtained for the purpose. Far from the serious assault that had been alleged, the second incident was confirmed to have been so trivial that the authorities had not bothered to record it.

The justifiable and perfectly understandable feelings of the Bulger family have always been that Thompson and Venables should have served time in an adult prison. It is unlikely that this would have been anything other than a retrograde step (for them and for society), but the sad truth was that no one wanted to believe either boy capable of reform. After an appeal to the European Court of Human Rights, they were released in 2001. There is a lifelong injunction in existence, which prohibits anyone from revealing their new identities. In January 2002, the *Mail*'s headlines 'Bulger Killer To Join Army' were followed by a story revealing that Jon, then eighteen years old, had applied to join a fighting regiment and would almost certainly be accepted. The normal rules excluding convicted murderers from the services would be waived. The paper asserted that it knew which regiment he had applied to join but added ruefully that it wasn't allowed to publish it. Robert, it said, had started an art course. It went on to explain that the pair were banned from Merseyside* for life and would be immediately sent back to prison if 'their behaviour warrants it'. From the tone of the article, the reader has the impression that the newspaper rather hopes it will.

---

* Liverpool's county.

6. MURDER ON HUNGERFORD BRIDGE

If you stand on the Thames Embankment between dusk and the early hours of the morning, London's great river undergoes two major transformations. As the daylight fades, there is the twinkling fairyland of early evening. The tourists and the culture seekers will be thronging towards the floodlit South Bank arts complex; the growing darkness is pricked with thousands of lights reflected in the water; the majestic dome of St Paul's Cathedral dominates the view further to the east, and the more warmly illuminated Houses of Parliament to the west. At dusk, this view is one of the most enchanting the capital has to offer.

After the Royal Festival Hall and the National Theatre have closed; after the wine bars and the clubs have served their last customers; as, one by one, the famous buildings are plunged into darkness, then the river becomes a black, surging chasm between the north and the south of the city. As you cross over one of its bridges and look down, you see nothing but blackness, but you can hear the monster lying in wait as it churns beneath you. You briefly recall its grim history, before going back to the lights of the modern world. They're now further from you than they were earlier and, perhaps unaccountably, you don't feel safe until you reach them.

At night, large parts of the banks of the river become the territory of the down-and-outs. Not very far away, in the concrete warren that leads down to Waterloo Station, is 'Cardboard City'. Here, in the tunnels and walkways, round the skateboarding arenas and on the steps, drugs and drink bring whatever kind of solace they may to those who do not know what rest is.

We used to know how a tramp ought to look: he or she was elderly – or at least appeared to be. They were sometimes drunk and incoherent. More often than not clutching their worldly possessions in stinking bags, they would stagger around the large cities during the day and sleep on park benches at night. If this stereotype ever could be relied upon, it can be no longer. Even the word 'tramp' is anachronistic, since there are too many different sorts of vagrant to general-ise about classification or habits. Now they may be of almost any age, from ten years upwards. Some of them are 'genuinely' homeless; some come from the bleak 'sink' housing estates. Many have, at appallingly early stages in their lives, encumbered themselves with severe addictions. They are not always obvious, either: they might look reasonably cared for; they may even be seen wearing designer clothes; but look at their eyes, and one may see the harsh cruelty of their lives reflected in them. Amongst their number are the thugs who will steal whatever they can get their hands on – those who think nothing of perpetrating violence, since violence of one form or another is all that they themselves have ever known. At night they will reclaim their territory, and turn the deserted back streets into danger zones. At night, they won't appeal to your sympathy; they will recognise your fear and use it against you.

The West End of London sucks in these people and holds them in its darker corners – on the edges of the bright, vibrant city that the tourists photograph and the rest of us inhabit. There are some who might spare a thought for their plight, but most of us pass by with a hurried excuse: 'Sorry, I don't have change.'

Timothy Baxter and Gabriel Cornish were intelligent, young, middle-class men: of the kind that would acknowledge the difficulties of the less fortunate, and might well have put their hands in their pockets whenever they could. They had promising futures ahead. Timothy (or 'Timo') was studying law, and Gabriel, sound engineering. That evening, 17 June 1998, had been a relaxing, enjoyable one. Timo was still carrying the skateboard he had been using earlier – as many others did – on the makeshift rinks on the South Bank. He and his friend had then gone out drinking in the 'Break for the Border' club just off Charing Cross Road, some twenty minutes' walk from the river. It was growing very late and they were going back to spend the night at Gabriel's mother's place; their way lay across the river and then on to Waterloo Station, where they would pick up a train to Peckham.

The possibility of danger might have entered either of their heads, but if it did they didn't dwell on it. Both were strong young men, and could be forgiven for thinking themselves safe against the few drunken louts they might have to walk past. Besides, Gabriel's rucksack didn't contain anything of great value. Neither had anything worth stealing, apart from a thin, silver bracelet – a present to Gabriel from his parents – and Timothy's skateboard. They walked down the deserted Villiers Street into Embankment Place. There they had to circumnavigate the closed underground station which normally allows direct access to the river. Once on the other side, they had a choice: they could walk a short distance to the reassuringly wide and well-lit Waterloo

Bridge, or they could take a chance on the narrow, darkened walkway which at that time bordered the Hungerford railway bridge.

This present year, 2002, sees the opening of a new Hungerford footbridge. The stinking, littered stone steps have been concreted over, and the new approach leads up to a modern, attractive thoroughfare. This new Hungerford Bridge is in accord with the clean, twenty-first century design of the nearby Millenium Wheel, its gleaming white supports rising above the Thames like the masts of majestic yachts. It's a far cry from the rusting, rattling structure that presented itself to the two students just four years earlier. Nevertheless, at 3.56 a.m. they decided that the extra walk was not equal to the estimated risk and so took this, the most direct route.

They were never to reach the other side. By sunrise Timo was dead, and Gabriel so severely traumatised that his life will always be blighted by the events of that terrible night.

Altogether, there were found to be six people responsible. The youngest was a fourteen-year-old boy, and the oldest just twenty-one. Though they knew each other (at least, some of them did), their 'friendship' was only a flimsy thing. It was simply the affiliation of like with like; there was little real loyalty or affection involved. These were street kids. It was true that two had homes to go to, but no one would have argued that their backgrounds were supportive. Their world was governed by the morality of the criminal: 'don't shit on your own doorstep, and don't grass on a mate'. If they had intelligence (one of them certainly did), then it was used only as a means to flout the rule of law; to find a place to sleep at night, and to acquire enough cash for their next hit of narcotics. Individually they might each have succeeded in climbing out of the abyss they shared, but together each fed off the other's disillusionment; they were united under a banner of mistrust of society, and the seeking of shallow pleasures.

Alan West was one who had a home he could go to. He also had a mother who cared about him. For Alan and his peers, a spell 'inside' was as common as a trip to the seaside is to more fortunate youngsters; violence was simply the way you settled scores, asserted your claims; after stealing or begging enough money to pay for them, drugs and drink were the normal way of relaxing.

At sixteen, Alan spent most of his time with older boys. They regarded him as good fun. He had demonstrated how much 'fun' he could be when he was only thirteen, and he and another lad broke into a house belonging to an elderly man. After knocking the occupant down the stairs (Alan's mother, Maggie, says the other boy did that), they stole cash from the old man's pocket. Alan was put into local authority care for eight months. Maggie, who sees her son as wrongly vilified, points out that he had seen that the old man had been hurt, and had considerately knocked on a neighbour's door before making his escape. She says, moreover, that she had always warned him about his dangerous lifestyle, and feared that he would end up dead or, at least, in very serious trouble. As it turned out, she was right.

Maggie is still at a loss to know why her son went so badly wrong. Part of her won't admit that he is quite as black as he is painted; the other part accepts the explanation he gave when asked why, when he had never gone without anything he needed, he found it necessary to steal and mug people. He told the court that there was 'a buzz in it'.

Unlike Alan, Sonni Reed was homeless. He spent his time in and around the West End, using as his base the London Connection, a day hostel for the homeless in Charing Cross. Six months previously, when he had first arrived there, he had been clean, tidy and amiable. As time went on, his appearance disintegrated, along with his hopes. He managed to make some money by begging, but would often find himself in trouble, sometimes becoming violent if a stranger dared to refuse him. Sonni's was a discouraging existence. It was the kind of life that every city has to offer those who miss the entrance to society.

He was friendly with a young man named John Riches ('John John') who, like Alan West (he knew Alan), had been brought up on the Aylesbury Estate. John John looked towards Sonni as the stronger character of the two for, though he himself was the eldest of the six, his emotional age was much younger than his 21 years. His mother had deserted her family when he was only fourteen. Two years later, his father had suffered a stroke and later died. John John had found the body too late for his desperate efforts at resuscitation to have any effect. Having had adoring parents, John John was thus left emotionally, as well as physically, bereft. His sister was, and still is, fiercely supportive of him, but even she couldn't take his emotional pain away. He demonstrated his anger by setting light to the bed in which his father had died. As a result, he was charged with arson and sent to a probation hostel.

These were the first three.

* * *

Sonni had been drinking and taking drugs that night. He met Alan and John John, and they spent some time in Leicester Square – a thriving tourist area surrounded by cinemas and with a garden at its centre where it's advisable to guard your wallet. This is a modern-day version of the London Charles Dickens wrote about, where the very rich and very poor rub shoulders. If any member of either class were asked to describe the city in which they lived, they would seem to talk about two completely different places.

The evening wore on, and became early morning. The three had no real plans and, finding the night more conducive to pleasure than the light of day, they were never about to waste it in sleep. They wandered over to Waterloo and, just before three o'clock, stopped off at an all-night off-licence to buy beer and vodka. They decided to go back to Leicester Square to drink it, and elected to go by the quickest route: across Hungerford Bridge. Tim and Gabriel, on the opposite bank, were about to do the same thing.

Types like West, Riches and Reed who hang around on the street, especially late at night, are best avoided. Once they have a few drinks inside them, hopeless, angry and violent, they will live up to their reputation as louts. As far as they are concerned, those who are not of their ilk are the enemy. Middle-class, well-spoken young men like the two who were walking towards them represent everything they never had and have no hope of getting. They frequently go about bawling foul insults at passers-by whose faces they don't like and who have come too close. Sometimes they refrain: this is on the occasions when they can't be bothered; when they have other things to think about or (more often than not) because our world, the world of privilege and politeness, is too dominant for them to be openly hostile. These are people you wouldn't 'want to bump into in a dark alley'; they are the ones nobody can reason with, who would not want to get acquainted with the stranger, because the stranger has always kept them at bay. Resentment festers in their nature like a deep neglected wound. Their power, their self-esteem, is sustained by brutal demonstrations of physical strength.

There are strategies we have all had to use at some time in our lives. We may try and ignore our fear, and walk a little faster, hoping that in three minutes or so, the unpleasantness will have receded into the distance; we may talk a little louder: forced chit-chat that is an obvious pretence at normality, a deliberate pretence at a nonchalance we cannot feel. Tim and Gabriel would have kept out of their way; would have thought better of walking too close to them, but, on Hungerford Bridge, there was nowhere else to go.

The three blocked their path. One of them demanded money. Here, in the darkness, with his mates to back him up, he didn't need to ask, as he would have done on a crowded pavement during daylight hours. His voice betrayed his feelings: he was enjoying this. These posh bastards knew exactly what he was going to do to them if they refused.

Gabriel tried to reason with them. He said they were robbing the wrong people: they had nothing valuable on them at all. It didn't work. The answer sounded too much like a ruse, and these lads had heard it a thousand times before. The idea that two young men with this kind of accent would be wandering round London without any cash was simply not credible. Tim and Gabriel attempted to push past and go on their way but, money or no money, their three antagonists were enjoying their encounter too much to let them go just yet. If nothing else, it was an entertaining way of wasting a quarter of an hour.

'No money?' one of them exclaimed in an incredulous tone. The pair had better think again! If they didn't hand over all they had, they would find themselves in the river. Tim and Gabriel were beginning to panic now. The skateboard wasn't worth much, and they couldn't think what else would pacify these people. What Gabriel had said was the truth: they were not carrying much cash. The only thing they had of any real value was Gabriel's silver chain, which he was loath to give up. Reasoning was evidently not going to work, though. 'Just leave us alone and let us pass. We haven't anything to give you and we don't want any trouble.' Something was riling their antagonists, and the two boys had no idea what it was. Was it their more refined voices; the way they were dressed, their middle-class attitude? It was all of these things yet (worse) it was nothing in particular.

West hadn't meant what he'd said about throwing them in the river, but his mind was fast going into autopilot. He repeated his threat, enjoying the reaction he was getting from his two companions as well as from the terrified students. He gripped Tim with one hand at the throat. Tim attempted to escape, so West punched him hard. The others did the same to Gabriel.

This assault might have been the conclusion of Gabriel and Tim's ordeal and, needless to say, it was a traumatic enough experience – senseless and vindictive. To be at the mercy of thugs doesn't cause only physical hurt; the psychological damage is just as bad. There is, during this kind of encounter, a growing feeling of helpless fury, a longing to go back just a few minutes, to when the world was the ordered, safe place that we usually feel it is.

At this juncture, three other people came onto the bridge from the north bank. The two boys felt a surge of relief as they saw their chance of escape. They called out: 'Can you help us? We're being robbed.'

It was the intervention of these three newcomers that brought about Timothy Baxter's death.

Antoinette (Toni) Blankson, Shaun Copeland and Cameron Sylas were heading towards Waterloo Station. It was around 4 a.m., and they were going home after an evening's entertainment.

Cameron was another regular at the London Connection Hostel. He was an educated person, and had had the ability at some point in his life to get back 'on track'. Although the hostel administrators thought him 'placid' – a 'gentle giant' – and though he had never caused any problems there, he had turned his back on conventional ways of earning a living and was known to the police for burglary and assault. He was eighteen years old.

Shaun and Toni were 'going out together'. Shaun was only fourteen and, like Toni, lived at home. He was no stranger to the West End at midnight. His friends were drop-outs, who spent most of their time feeding their addictions. As he later told the police: 'That's all they ever do – just rob people and go and buy drugs.'

Toni Blankson comes across as a sullen young girl who, having reached sixteen, considered herself to be an adult. Her young boyfriend was not a serious relationship, so far as she was concerned. Like him, she sought the company of older, more stimulating people. These were often dangerous types. Her mother had (at least to some extent) neglected her parental responsibilities. Toni, she thought, was old enough to know what she was doing, and she could look after herself.

These three had also spent the evening in and around Leicester Square where, no doubt, they had already seen West, Riches and Reed. They were probably drunk, probably 'stoned'. The instinct that took over when Tim and Gabriel called out to them for help was pure animal bloodlust. Without pause for reflection, they gleefully joined in the attack.

Shaun went in first, throwing a punch at Tim's head, but he missed. He immediately transferred his attentions to Gabriel, hitting him full in the face and causing him to fall to the ground. As he fell, and as consciousness left him, Gabriel heard one of them say yet again: 'Let's throw them in the river. It will be fun.'

John Riches has it that, as soon as Gabriel was on the ground, Sonni started to stamp on his head. Either West or Riches joined in and then – 'like they'd done it a million times before' – they hauled the boys over the four-foot barrier and let their senseless bodies fall into the Thames. They were laughing as they did it. From later comments on police tapes, it seems that at least some of them thought their victims were already dead:

Police: Did anyone say like, you know, 'Oh my God, we've gotta call the police.' Did you say anything like that?
Toni: I did say to Cameron and Shaun that it wasn't worth throwing the bodies over: bodies float.[1]

We do not know for certain which of them did it, nor how many of them were fully involved. We do not know whether any of them protested about what was done by the others, though it seems unlikely. Each of the six blamed the others in the group. According to their conflicting statements, not one of them did anything other than watch in amazement as everybody (except themselves) indulged in this brutality. John Riches went so far as to say he thought that to laugh at such an atrocity was 'sick'. CCTV footage, showing him smiling and joking just after the murder, proves he was not of this opinion at the time.

There is a primeval part of the human consciousness that feels sanctions for one's own actions are to be found in membership of a pack. It is entirely possible that none of those individuals would have contemplated murder had they not been together. It is possible that none of them actually initiated the killing in a deliberate way: the scent of blood is, we are told, enough to drive a pack of animals into a frenzy. Questions of rational motivation, either for the initial attack or for the subsequent drowning, seem superfluous: a young man died that night, for no reason that any sane person would see. It's not enough to say he was in the wrong place at the wrong time; it's not enough to explain the hatred that killed him as being a result of deprivation, or intoxicated stupor. This was a monstrous, revolting, and totally gratuitous act.

The six, having sated their immediate need for entertainment, split into their two groups of three and went their separate ways. They didn't seem to have much consideration for their two victims. Could they have supposed the boys were dead before they were thrown into the water? Could they seriously have thought there would be nothing to connect them to the killings? What precautions they took were rudimentary: they remembered to cover their faces as they passed the CCTV cameras at the ends of the bridge but could not hope to avoid being recorded elsewhere. It is from the CCTV cameras that we know what they did next.

Their terrible crime apparently forgotten, Cameron, Toni and Shaun are seen smiling as they come up the escalator. Asked about this later, Toni denied it. 'No,' she said. It was just Cameron who was 'making silly dumb jokes ... about vegetables'.[2] The two younger ones were certainly not displaying any of the reactions one would expect. They were taken up with each other, and are seen kissing fondly.

West, Reed and Riches went on to steal someone's wallet. The man gave chase and thumped West in the stomach before calling the police.

Meanwhile, Gabriel had regained consciousness. The rucksack on his back was keeping him afloat. He was, after thirty minutes in the cold water, already suffering from hypothermia. He was being swept upstream past the Houses of Parliament. In his confused state he thought he saw Tim on the bank waving to him. He began to cry out and was heard by a man on his way to work, who was able to alert the emergency services. Timothy Baxter's body was found on the shore, 36 hours later.

It seems that, alone among his killers, John John Riches suffered pangs of conscience, although it was only after he had been arrested that they became manifest. Left to himself in a cell, he burst into tears. An officer asked him what the matter was. 'They've thrown some guy off the bridge,' Riches said. 'Sonni's thrown some guy off the bridge.'[3]

If the policeman's recollection is accurate, it seems odd that Riches made reference to only one person and it is, perhaps, significant that he names Sonni Reed as the gang leader. We will never know whether it was remorse or fear that prompted him but, on the Aylesbury Estate, your reason for reporting an incident doesn't matter much: no matter what hideous activity you're involved in, the golden rule is that you don't 'grass' on a mate. From then on, as far as the people that had mattered to him were concerned, John John Riches was beyond the pale.

These people have a morality different from the rest of us. We may find it mind-boggling that any other consideration would override the fact that they had thrown two helpless young men into the Thames. In their primitive world, the police are the natural foe. Any person who helps them in the slightest way is guilty of treachery, no matter what other imagined qualities they may have. In BBC television's *Crime Kids*, Maggie, Alan West's mother, who – despite the evidence to the contrary – insisted her son was not a killer, says: 'It's an unwritten law: you don't grass on people – because if it wasn't for the fact that John John Riches said that, they would never have picked Alan up. They would never have connected him over there. They didn't have any what I would call proper photographs of Alan, face-wise. As I say, someone's gotta pay for it.'[4]

She wasn't blind to his faults. She said she knew he was 'no angel'. It's a term often used by those who speak for young criminals. It is meant to persuade us that the speaker is objective enough to be relied upon when they whitewash over a crime or (as with Maggie) simply deny that their son could possibly have been part of it. 'No angel' is not really a pejorative phrase. It is almost an endearment. Can we blame a mother for refusing to accept that her son is capable of murder? Maggie was not articulate enough to express fully the complex and contrary emotions she must have felt. She has to live by the code and, in this case, the code says that while to be a thug and a murderer is acceptable in some cases, to be a 'grass' is unforgivable.

Alan West's sister, on the other hand, apparently thought her brother's statement should have absolved him of his responsibility in the matter. In common with just about everybody else who spoke for the six, she vehemently denied the possibility that her brother might have been involved. 'It was out of his hands,' she said. 'What happened on that bridge was completely out of his hands and he's the one that's gotta live with it.' She went on, with some incredulity in her voice, to point out that her brother 'can't win': he has suffered for being a grass as well as being stigmatised as a murderer.

John Riches himself (perhaps to his credit) did at least realise something of the enormity of what had happened. 'I'm not a grass,' he said, 'but I don't keep secrets; nothing like that anyway. I couldn't hold that in, it would have just played about in my mind.'

Their perfunctory efforts to hide their faces from the CCTV cameras had not been successful: Shaun Copeland and Cameron Sylus were known to the police, and it didn't take long to arrest them. Toni Blankson proved more difficult to find. It was another two weeks before she was picked up. During that time, her five friends were telling five different stories. Their code of ethics apparently frowned only on the original 'grass'. When the story was out, they unashamedly incriminated each other.

Shaun Copeland: I was just walking around, 'cos I was scared.
Police Officer: Outside of the group?
Shaun Copeland: Yeah.
Police Officer: What was Antoinette doing?
Shaun Copeland: She was just running round going: 'Yeah, yeah, do it some more.' Like it was funny, you know.

Police Officer: What, egging the boys on?

Shaun Copeland: Yeah.

Shaun's mother: I just don't believe what I just heard. Do you understand? That was somebody's son. Do you understand? His poor mum!

Police Officer: Did you assault, hit, kick in any way, shape or form the two people?

Alan West: No.

Police Officer: Not at all?

Alan West: Not at all. Sonni kept going: 'That's the ninth person I've killed.'[5]

Toni added to these statements her own – sixth – version of events. Her tone of voice was full of feigned astonishment at her so-called friends' mendaciousness and equally unbelievable wonder that they dared tell untruths in the wake of such a grave matter.

'I was scared,' she said at one point, making it sound as if this fictitious fear were not merely mild apprehension. 'I didn't think they'd go as far as murder though.'

Unless all the group could be proved to be involved in the crime, it was going to be difficult to bring a case against any one of them, since not one of their stories could be trusted over any of the others and it was probable that all six of them were lying. However, the fact that they had been present at the killing was, in the end, sufficient grounds for conviction. The law has it that non-intervention in such an attack is tantamount to being a consenting party. None of them had denied they were at the scene of the crime, and consequently all six were found guilty. They received sentences of between twelve and sixteen years. Shaun Copeland and Toni Blankson were detained at Her Majesty's Pleasure and the rest received prison sentences.

John Riches' sister maintains that he is full of remorse, but is also keen to point out that there must be part of him that wishes he hadn't volunteered his story. As far as she is concerned, it is because of this mistake that he is now locked away; that he cannot ever return to the Aylesbury Estate where he is now known as a 'grass' and for the fact that he has (unfairly in her opinion) been labelled as a murderer.

Gabriel Cornish gave up his studies. His hopes for the future were taken from him that night on Hungerford Bridge. Timothy Baxter's grieving parents buried their son and, with him, their happiness.

Not one of the six killers had any hope of gaining more than a few trifles from what they did that night. They let themselves be taken over by an unrestrained lust for cruelty, which is, perhaps, all the more shocking to read about because there is a potential for it in all of us. Timothy Baxter and Gabriel Cornish were seen by them as alien and what is alien, they felt, must be attacked. It is this selfsame delusion that dehumanises the foreigner or gay person in the eyes of certain people; that can persuade one to forget that any animal feels pain. When in its grip, there is little chance that our humanity will be able to show its face.

Gabriel Cornish and his family have never spoken publicly about that night. He remains haunted by the savagery of the attack and the loss of his friend.

7. THE BODY IN THE CANAL

In the fairy tale, Hansel and Gretel did not know that the old lady who invited them into her house was really a witch and that she intended to kill and eat them. The following history also involves an old lady who allows two children into her house but, if we look for the good and the evil, the characters are completely reversed. Here it is the children – this time two girls – who are disgustingly malicious, and the old lady their blameless victim.

Oldham is situated about six miles north of Manchester. It lies on the lower slopes of the Pennine hills, and was once a flourishing cotton-manufacturing town. Since the mills closed down in the late 60s and early 70s, parts of Oldham have become run down, and may seem depressing to a visitor.* Recent race riots have done nothing to enhance its image, and a visitor can be at once drawn to the friendliness of many of the inhabitants (regardless of their ethnic origin) and put off by the deep, resentful suspicion of some others. The cosy

---

* My view was challenged by an inhabitant who writes: 'Oldham has a goodly share of deprived areas. In fact, it is listed quite high in the national list of deprived areas. In spite of this unassailable fact, it has made a fair recovery from the decline of cotton-yarn manufacture, and in spite of huge council debts incurred in the wake of desirable developments and money 'wasted' on 'harebrained' schemes that have now been demolished, it is not a town in decline any more, but rather a fairly forward-looking town, with an important contribution to industrial output of all kinds.'

image of northern England as a friendly, honest, hard-working community of terraced houses and cobbled streets became obsolete decades ago; possibly this impression was always a chimera. If sturdy old ladies in hair-nets ever did offer no-nonsense advice to grubby but open-hearted children, they do so no longer. Throughout the north – throughout all Britain – a great number of the elderly live in fear of youngsters who are perceived to be more likely to carry a knife than a catapult.

Failsworth is an 'urban district' of Oldham. Not being very far away from pleasant countryside, it could be said to be a good address. Though it has come down in appearance a bit in parts (some of it looks rather shabby), much of it is still a reasonably pleasant part of the town, and there are plenty of people who are happy enough to own property there. They could be forgiven for not taking much time to consider why young rowdies (of both sexes) rampage around the neighbourhood. The usual simplistic views seem to fit, and those are the ones you'd hear being expressed today: 'It's the parents who are to blame. My father wouldn't have let me get away with half of what they do'; 'Not enough discipline at home'; 'It's drugs – and I'm not just talking about a bit of a puff, like in my day – they're on heroin and crack, and they don't care how they get it'; 'It's single mothers. They just breed to get money off the Social [Security], and then they let their kids run riot'; 'If there wasn't so much of it [violence] on television, it would help.'[1]

In September 1998, two of these children crossed the line from delinquency to criminality. They were both girls, and both were under sixteen. Their names were not made public at the time of their trial because the courts decided (against a ruling by the judge, Mr Justice

Sachs) that they should continue to be referred to simply as Child A and Child B. This decision was roundly condemned and was overturned in November 2002 by the Lord Chief Justice, Lord Woolf.

The older girl, Lisa Healey, was said by one defence psychiatrist to be suffering from post-traumatic stress disorder after a campaign of terror had been waged against her family. This happened in 1995, when they were living in south Manchester in an area known as Longsight.

Lisa's mother, Margaret, had witnessed an armed robbery at a post office. Expressions of resentment over the help she had provided for the prosecution were prompt and terrible. She was beaten up and 'slashed'. Lisa's brother was stabbed and, before her eyes, her father was hit with a baseball bat. Lisa herself, aged only eleven at the time, was ostracised and bullied at school, so much so that she was moved four times in attempts to cure the problem. Unsurprisingly, this relatively normal child soon became a truant. She turned to drink, cigarettes and narcotics; she ran away from home more than once and, fully aware of the risks she was taking, would willingly accept lifts from strangers. She became aggressive, and an expert liar. She learnt how to manipulate those with authority over her. This was clearly a child bent on a collision with disaster. Soon, shoplifting and vandalism were added to her record, and she was even convicted of affray. By 1997, when she was thirteen, she'd been cautioned five times. Perhaps the vengeful attacks on her family were responsible for her delinquency; but whatever the reason for it, her adolescent personality emerged in a most unpleasant form.

Sarah Davey wore the 'good girl gone wrong' stereotype more convincingly than Lisa. Debra Davey blamed the events of that summer on her daughter's friend. She said that Sarah was well behaved until the pair met. She alleged that Lisa had 'a hold' on Sarah, and had corrupted her. Sarah had been in trouble before, but not in any serious way. She had once stolen some bread, just for a dare, and she had a reputation for answering back (or 'being mouthy', as it is described locally). She was a good student at school, and though her headmaster said she was usually friendly and agreeable, she had been punished on numerous occasions for bullying. On other occasions, she had had to go to hospital after becoming intoxicated, and had been involved in fights. She was naturally reserved, but was on the right side of average attainment and, again according to her headteacher, was a very friendly girl. 'There were never any complaints about her work,' he said.[2] She was slightly younger than her co-accused.

The two attended the same school; they lived near to each other, and both seemed to have a need to assert themselves as delinquents. It seems that Lisa 'took a shine' to Sarah, and they became friends. It wasn't long before other youngsters recognised that the pair were best avoided.

Their pairing-up marked the onset of a whole round of disturbing behaviour. No doubt it alarmed some people, but not so much that any drastic steps were taken to curb it. According to DCI Keith Dillon, who was one of the men who led the investigation into their actions, Lisa at least could have been said to be 'out of control'.[3]

Most children are impatient to wear the trappings of adulthood; the difference was, these two weren't prepared to wait. Not old enough to know about the burden of adult responsibility, or to care about the correlation between effort and reward, they simply wanted to break away from adult control; from school and exams – in short, from being what they in fact were: children. In Lisa, Sarah saw a person who would show her a fast way to independence. Lisa saw in Sarah an ally in her fight against the world. Freedom from constraint became their *raison d'être*; the result was a predictable run of petty thieving and other anti-social behaviour. They also developed a taste for casual sex, and talked about owning their own home, where parental restraints could not interfere with their fun. At the beginning of September 1998, they were caught shoplifting in the company of Lisa's younger male cousin, who they were using as a decoy. The next day they were stopped while carrying a martial arts weapon, and one of them was cautioned. It was still being considered whether to charge the other with possession of an offensive weapon when they ran away from home together. They spent some time wandering the streets, but didn't stray very far from the area in which they both lived. Their respective parents became worried over their absence, and reported them missing. On Tuesday 22 September 1998 [some reports have it as Wednesday 23], behaving very much like any other children who want to make their point without sacrificing too much comfort, they turned up at the home of Sarah's grandfather, and asked if they could stay the night. No doubt wise to the desire of young people to escape parental strictures sometimes, and thinking it would be safer for them to stay with him than to go running off elsewhere, he agreed. He might not have been so ready to accommodate Sarah's new friend had he known what was said later: Lisa asked if he lived alone. When told that he did, she said to Sarah, 'Should I kill him and then we can have his house?'[4]

Sarah didn't take this question seriously. Maybe she thought it was a daring and outrageous thing to say: just the sort of thing she had come to expect from Lisa. She admired this kind of audacity. It showed that Lisa wasn't bound by the same kind of boring, petty rules that everyone else seemed to obey. It was part of what she found exciting about her. In the end, it seems unlikely that they actually slept at the old man's house that night, or if they did, it wasn't for much of it. The reports are confused, mainly because the story had become mangled in the two girls' desperate attempts to put the blame onto each other, but we do know that a truck driver picked them up at about five o'clock on the Wednesday morning. They were so drunk they could hardly stand. He took both of them with him to Wales, where he made a delivery before driving back to Oldham. The girls told him they were sixteen years old (the British age of consent); one of them said she was pregnant. For some reason (maybe to elicit sympathy) they both claimed to be in care. The truck driver left them in Failsworth five hours later, at about ten o'clock. Whether this was an innocent trip or not can only be guessed at, as can the after-effects of having drunk so much alcohol (and maybe taken other drugs as well).

During that time, as they enjoyed the adventure of being runaways, they may well have made high-flown plans for the future. Perhaps they thought they might end up living with the truck driver; maybe even getting pregnant by him. They didn't have much idea about the realities of such a situation: everything was a game to them. They may have discussed running off to a big city; being famous criminals: kids' fantasy stuff. In nine out of ten cases, it's harmless and silly, but this was the tenth case.

Later that morning they met a Mrs Lilley outside a health centre a few hundred yards from where she lived at 17 West Street.

Lillian Lilley was perceived as an eccentric by those who knew her. She was generally well liked, although she may have invited a certain amount of derision because of her habit of muttering to herself, and the fact that she would always wear her bright red raincoat, even when the sun was shining. 'A nice lady,' her former neighbour, Mr Kershaw, said. 'She was easy to get on with and the children liked her. She would try and befriend them and most of them would do jobs for her.'[5] Those who did would never know how she was going to be on any particular day. There were days when she would simply ignore them, and others when she would shout, irritably driving them away from her door. There were times, though, when she would offer them sweets and crisps in return for their doing small chores such as tidying her garden. 'It was just a few who would cause trouble,' Mr Kershaw said. 'Especially those two.'[6]

Sarah, who lived close to West Street, would certainly have known of Mrs Lilley for some time, even if they had not actually been on speaking terms. Everybody in the neighbourhood knew of Mrs Lilley, the oddity. Another adult neighbour asserted that the old lady had been afraid of harassment; that she had only given children treats in order to stop their bullying. They would, she said, hammer on her door, throw stones at her windows and shout obscenities. In fact, there appear to be several different opinions current about Mrs Lilley's character and her relationship with local children, but she was certainly thought of as an oddity by everyone, and while she befriended some, it is likely there were others in addition to Sarah and Lisa who caused her trouble.

It is not at all clear whether the pair wheedled their way into her home, or whether they bullied her into taking them back. Mrs Lilley, when they finally met, may or may not have recognised them as the same girls who had taken the heads off flowers in her front garden. Even if she had known who they were, she may have been willing to forgive them, but it seems more likely that Lisa and Sarah saw her as easy prey, and felt no need to make overtures.

Lisa – probably the one who had suggested that the girls run away together – would be keen to enhance her already influential image in the eyes of her companion. Both would be either 'hung over', or still actually drunk. It's easy to imagine them giggling at just about anything in order to cover their fatigue, neither wanting the other to suspect that she had any doubts about this being the kind of adventure that they ought to relish. Doubts were cowardly and weak; doubts were for kids.

At this point, Sarah spots the 'madwoman' from West Street. As usual, she is wearing her bright red plastic mac, and is muttering to herself. She reminds Lisa of the last time she threatened to call the police to complain about some minor cheek they'd given her. The two girls nearly collapse with mirth on seeing the woman's faltering attempts to cross the road. Sarah once again gives a childish, malicious description of the old lady's character. If, like many of the other local children, she knows the real Mrs Lilley and is aware of how unfair her comments are, she doesn't give any hint. This is another opportunity to show that she's on Lisa's side in their battle against the adult world.

'She's mental,' she says. 'She thinks she rules that street, but she's just a dirty old tramp.'

Mrs Lilley still hasn't managed to get across the road. Lisa suggests they go up and give her a hard time. It will be fun and besides, they might be able to get some cash out of her. She yells across the road but Mrs Lilley pretends not to hear. Lisa is now determined, and Sarah, despite slight misgivings, is not going to let the side down. They both rush over to Mrs Lilley and Sarah, ignoring her indignant protests, starts looking through the old woman's shopping bags. To prove how tough she really is, Lisa swears directly into the old lady's face. Mrs Lilley tries to snatch her shopping back, but Lisa facetiously offers to carry it for her. It's a clever, domineering ploy: one that would be familiar to any playground victim. A refusal could be taken by the girls for a snub, and would therefore be an excuse for aggression. Acceptance, on the other hand, would give the two tormenters permission to carry on under the thin guise of friendship. Mrs Lilley thanks them with a diplomatic show of politeness, and says that she can manage on her own. Her voice trembles slightly, and the girls notice this indication of fear. She begins to move across the road and the two girls begin to follow, Lisa nudging Sarah and winking at her. They know where she lives, they say. They were thinking of going towards West Street, anyway.

They can see that Mrs Lilley is trying to hurry home without making it seem too obvious. They keep up their pretence of cordiality along the way. Everything they say is tinged with menace but, if taken at face value, devoid of any ill intent.

'Why do you always wear that coat?'

'Are your bags heavy?'

'I think you ought to give us a drink. We're thirsty.'

Mrs Lilley delights them by continuing to mutter to herself all the way. They find this inordinately amusing, in fact, and don't disguise the fact. By the time they reach 17 West Street, the old lady is a bundle of nerves, and the two girls are pumping with adrenalin.

'We want a drink,' Sarah says, pleased at her own bravado. She looks at Lisa and sees approval in her face. She pushes her luck just a little bit further. 'Give us a drink and we'll go. We're thirsty, and we haven't got anywhere to live.'

Mrs Lilley says she knows very well where they live and she's going to complain to their parents just as soon as she sees them. This is only a bluff, and the girls know it. Mrs Lilly might be vaguely aware of where Sarah's house is, but neither of them is really known to her. Besides, what have they done that would get them into any more trouble than they are in already? Lisa becomes a little more threatening in her manner. She has to at least match Sarah's boldness all the time or risk losing status – her 'cred'.

'If you don't give us a drink, we'll just stay here on your doorstep. You can't stop us – it's a free country.'

She takes a bottle of shampoo from Mrs Lilley's bag and squirts it at her. Sarah privately thinks this is going a bit too far, but still doesn't want to break rank. In order to keep in with Lisa, she pokes Mrs Lilley in the ribs, and says simply: 'Yeah.'

They are seen by a young boy who will later testify against them in court.

Mrs Lilley reluctantly allows them into her house, and tells them to stay in the kitchen while she puts the kettle on. They ignore her instruction, and go into the living room. Lisa immediately looks around for any valuables. Sarah is already going through some photographs and papers in one of the sideboard drawers. Lisa also takes a handful of these as Mrs Lilley comes stumbling over to where they are standing, and tries to take them from the girls' hands. Lisa runs behind the sofa and waves them at her, daring her to make another attempt.

The two girls are unassailable now, and they know it. If this old woman had any means of contacting anybody outside, they are sure that she would have done it by now. She can threaten all she wants; they are going to have some fun and, as Lisa has already whispered to Sarah, they will 'nick' some money before they go.

Whichever version one is to believe of what happened next is not very important. Sarah's original statement seems to imply that everything that happened from then on was in quick succession. It seems more likely that the two girls left Mrs Lilley alone for some time, and returned later on. Less likely is that they may somehow have managed to win her round, and then been given permission to stay for a short while. (They had, several times before, claimed to be pregnant and may, after all, have been able to wheedle their way into her sympathies.) Mrs Lilley's son lived in Queensland, and she would often tell the local youngsters about him, and his new life at the other end of the world. Sarah later excused the old lady's absence by saying that she had gone off to Australia. It is entirely possible that she knew about this connection already, but if she didn't, then at some point during their stay Mrs Lilley must have engaged in casual conversation with them. It doesn't mean they were any the less callous. Conversation of this nature, if it was engaged in at all, was simply an instrument of their duplicity. Their overriding interest at this point was surely to obtain money by any means possible. We know that from Thursday onwards, they were using Mrs Lilley's phone; they made 258 calls between then and Sunday. Clearly, with or without the old lady's permission, knowledge or presence, they were using the house as their own from the day after they first entered it.

The next witness evidence (from another young neighbour) tells us that one of the pair was seen in the house that Thursday and, at that point, was not at all keen to let people know of her presence. When the visitor looked through the letterbox, she ducked down behind the sofa. By the next day, however, the girls were being quite brazen about their presence in the house. They told several people that they were Mrs Lilley's grandchildren, and again trotted out the story about being pregnant.

A Mrs Duran remembers seeing Mrs Lilley alive and well at about 4 p.m. on the Friday: 'I stopped and talked to her briefly and she told me she was going to my house to post my daughter's fifteenth birthday card. She looked very clean, and her hair was fine. Her appearance took me back a bit.'[7]

Several different assumptions can be made from this statement but only one makes sense of the remarks about Mrs Lilley's appearance. Mrs Duran could have been mistaken about the day, or Mrs Lilley might willingly have been giving house room to the two girls, and thought, by then, that they were trustworthy enough to leave alone in her home. A more likely explanation is that the two girls had left, at least temporarily, and Mrs Lilley had spruced herself up in order to regain some dignity after being abused by them.

If they ever did leave after that first encounter, we also know that they returned at the earliest on Thursday, and no later than Friday. Yet another neighbour saw Lisa in the backyard at noon on Friday. Lisa was seen running out of the house, and Mrs Lilley was heard shouting: 'Go on! Get out!' Lisa didn't seem concerned about this. She simply went back into the house and closed the door. The witness didn't pay much attention to any of this. She had seen many children around that particular house and, in any case, she wasn't even certain it was Lisa that Lily was shouting at; it could just as easily have been one of the cats.

At her trial, Sarah was to spend seven days under cross-examination. Although her testimony cannot be relied upon absolutely and some details must be viewed as questionable, something like the following took place:

Lisa asks to use the toilet. This, of course, would mean one or the other of the two would have to be left unsupervised long enough for her to be able to steal something. Although they have abused her hospitality and, we can imagine, been anything but polite guests, the two girls both know the old lady will not be brave enough to call their bluff and show them the door. She doesn't demur at the request, and Lisa goes upstairs, unattended.

After some time Mrs Lilley, certain that the girl is up to no good, becomes agitated. She doesn't like the prospect of leaving Sarah alone in the living room either, but feels that she has no option but to see what Lisa is doing upstairs. Shortly afterwards, there is the sound of a scuffle.

Sarah must be feeling a little frightened by now. Lisa has been caught in some dishonest act or other and, though her friend has always made light of being in trouble with the police, she, Sarah, does not relish the idea. This is big stuff that doesn't involve just a ticking off from her parents or the headmaster – people are sent away for stealing from other people's houses.

She may contemplate running away without Lisa, but knowing that she would be implicated anyway, and still not wanting to get on the wrong side of Lisa, she eventually goes to see what is happening.

She climbs the staircase slowly, not knowing whether to call out to Lisa or not. She half-whispers 'Lisa! What are you doing?' Everything is very quiet. Sarah pauses at the top of the stairs. She doesn't know whether to be relieved or frightened when Lisa appears from one of the bedrooms, and beckons her to come in.

Mrs Lilley is lying on the floor moaning softly. She seems to be scarcely conscious. Her mouth is open, and her breath comes in great heaving gulps, followed by a rasping sound as she expels air. Her face is very pale, and her leg is in an awkward, unnatural position. Although Sarah can tell that her friend is very worried indeed, Lisa is pretending to be nonchalant. The only clues to her real attitude are the pitch of her voice, the speed of her speech and the fact that her hands are trembling slightly. She wouldn't want it to be known that her anxiety was obvious and Sarah is wise enough to discern that she, too, must adopt the same response. She may have already betrayed her anxiety when she came into the room and first saw the old lady, for she gasped and took a minute or two to collect herself. Now, however, her brain has fully engaged, and she is unquestioningly following Lisa's lead.

'She's not dead,' Lisa says, as she puts some jewellery into her pocket. Then she forces a smile. 'She caught me taking her horrible necklaces. As if I'd want to wear these.'

She holds up a string of beads and poses, holding them round her neck. Then, looking every inch the cool, confident thief, she stuffs them in her pocket and adds, 'I suppose they might be worth a fiver.'

'What are we going to do with her?' Sarah asks. She doesn't want to appear too concerned but she is, nevertheless, very worried about the old lady's breathing. Her mind is racing with the options that present themselves in the space of a few seconds, the most practical one being (as she hopes Lisa will agree) to ring for an ambulance and then get as far away from the house as possible. Even if they do this, she knows in the back of her mind that there will still be difficulties. Mrs Lilley had said that she knew them and knew where their parents lived. They hadn't believed her at the time, but there is always the possibility that she was speaking the truth. Sarah feels sick. She knows she is in trouble right up to her neck, and there isn't going to be an easy way out of it.

'We'll tie her up and stay here for a bit,' Lisa announces. It's the last thing Sarah wants to do. She protests: 'We can't do that! Somebody will find out and they'll send the police round. We've got to get away. Can't we just go?'

Lisa reminds her that they've always wanted their own house; now they have the chance to take one, she's not going to let the opportunity pass her by. If, she says accusingly, Sarah is too 'chicken' to stay with her then she can fuck off back home.

The two girls have now sealed their fate and that of Mrs Lilley. Neither can back out of this diabolic game without seeming cowardly or treacherous. Mrs Lilley is injured very badly and, without help, will be in serious difficulties. Were she to recover, both of the girls would be in serious trouble. The alternative is too much to contemplate, but at the back of their minds is the growing notion that if she were to die, it could feasibly be perceived as a natural death: perhaps the result of a fall.

Mrs Lilley has suddenly gone very quiet. Lisa runs over and presses her ear close to Mrs Lilley's mouth. A relieved look appears on her face. It's one of the few genuine signs of concern that she has shown so far. 'She's still breathing,' is all she says.

The two then start arguing. Sarah remembers seeing where Mrs Lilley had tried to hide her purse in a kitchen drawer. She says she is going to get it, take the money and get out. Lisa follows her down the stairs, telling her not to be so stupid. They can take the money and whatever else they find in the house, and still stay there, for a few weeks at least. They could have some fun, and, after that, go somewhere else where nobody would ever find them. Somebody would discover Mrs Lilley in time and they would think she had died on her own. It is the first time the possibility of Mrs Lilley's death has been voiced. Sarah remembers what Lisa said about her grandfather on Tuesday night. It had seemed daring then. Now they are faced with the very real possibility of being responsible for someone else's death. This doesn't seem the same at all. It seems – she can't put the thought into words, but she knows underneath what her conscience is telling her – it seems wrong.

They are in the kitchen. The purse is there in the drawer. Sarah says they will share the amount fifty-fifty. Lisa says they must do that with whatever they get from now on because they're going on the run, and they will have to depend on each other. The game seems, briefly, exciting again, until they remember the presence of Mrs Lilley upstairs. 'What will we do when she wakes up?' Sarah says.

'Kill her,' Lisa replies.

They have taken a knife from the kitchen drawer – neither knows exactly why. They go up the stairs cautiously, half-remembered scenes from horror films coming into their minds. They know the old lady is not a threat to either of them but they are still unaccountably afraid. When they get to the bedroom they are relieved to find that nothing has changed. Mrs Lilley is still lying where they left her; she is still breathing.

They are wondering what to do next when she stirs. Her eyes are half open, and she moans. Without thinking, Lisa grabs a pillow and covers Mrs Lilley's face. Her victim kicks and struggles, this time more strongly than she did before. Sarah jabs at her legs with the knife and Lisa pushes down with the pillow to stifle the resulting cry.

Some horrible animal instinct has taken over now. They are taking it in turns to stab at Mrs Lilley's legs, and to hold the pillow over her face. When she is quiet again, there is a dreadful silence for what seems like an hour. It's probably only a few moments.

Slowly Sarah removes the pillow. She's not sure whether she's relieved or not when she hears a painful, shallow breathing coming from the old lady's pale lips. Lisa has an idea. They will gag Mrs Lilley and leave her tied up in the room. The practicalities of such an action aren't an issue: it seems as good a thing to do as anything else.

They find a bandage in one of the bedroom drawers and, propping Mrs Lilley up into a sitting position, force it into her mouth. One holds it tight, very tight, while the other ties it in a secure bow. The gag dislodges Mrs Lilley's false teeth, and she chokes. The choking brings her briefly back to consciousness and she starts to struggle again. Later on they don't remember which one of them puts the pillow over her face for the last time, but when they finally take it off, Mrs Lilley has stopped choking, stopped struggling: she is dead.

'We've killed her,' Sarah says with something approaching wonderment. She feels sick and extremely frightened. She somehow hopes her friend will have some practical answer to all this, but subconsciously she knows that Lisa has no idea what to do and that she never had much of an idea from the very beginning.

Lisa shrugs and gets up. 'Let's see what's here,' she says. 'We might as well take what's going.'

Sarah claims that she also joked: 'Lily, don't come and haunt me.' Allegedly, she also said, 'We can have her house, we can live in this house.'[8] Then she warned her friend: 'I am going to seriously damage you if you say anything.'

Once Mrs Lilley had been murdered, it seems that both girls pushed conscience into the background and set about having a good time in 'their' new house. They set off across the road to spend the old lady's money. As well as toothpaste and deodorant, they also bought childish comfort food. A boy recalls seeing Coco Pops in their bag. He was suspicious about this, because he knew that Mrs Lilley would never buy anything like that. Sarah has it that they then crossed the main road and went for a short walk by the canal. It was here that Lisa had an idea about how they might get rid of the body.

At about nine o'clock that evening, back at West Street, she came into the living room with one of the huge wheeled bins that the local council provides for the removal of household waste. She then told Sarah that they were getting rid of the body now. Between them, they wrapped Mrs Lilley's remains in a blanket and somehow managed to pull her downstairs. Lying the bin on its side on the living-room floor, the two of them 'kicked and pushed' the corpse into it. Then followed the part of this sad tale that has made it notorious: two young girls, still not sixteen years old, with their recently murdered victim in a rubbish bin, trundled it through the streets of Failsworth looking for somewhere to dump the body.

They were seen by several people. One passer-by recalled one of them saying, 'I can't believe we're doing this,' to which the other replied, 'Yeah, whatever.' They were giggling, probably out of nervousness rather than, as has been implausibly suggested, that they were finding the whole affair amusing. Their route took them down West Street, across the road, past the health centre where they had met their victim, and through a car park by the Co-operative 'Shopping Giant' store. There would have been lots of people about at that time of night, especially when they reached Oldham Road, but though comments were made, nobody actually approached them to ask what they were up to. Teen-agers who looked as if they were 'up to no good' were best left alone. On the main road, immediately adjacent to the canal bridge, there is a wine bar. A security guard recalled seeing the two as they struggled down the stone steps to the canal bank. He made some comment about the weight of the bin and, though he must have guessed where it was going to end up, he made no effort to stop them. He remembered them reappearing, without the bin, about thirty minutes later.

The Rochdale Canal has been cleaned up regularly since 1998. As in the distant past, boats are once more able to travel it, but before then it was an ignominious place to end up. It had been for years a dumping place for any kind of rubbish. Ducks struggled through its cluttered waters, somehow adding to the depressing effect. Though its potential could be seen through all the mess and neglect, one could be forgiven for supposing that any efforts to improve its decrepit state would be reversed as soon as they were put into effect. Mrs Lilley had been dead for three days when her corpse was found in the rubbish bin, partly submerged and hardly discernible amongst the general debris. It was bent double and, strangely – perhaps as a sick joke or perhaps because her killers had simply thrown it away – a photo of the old lady's son as a baby had been tossed in there with her. Mrs Lilley was wrapped in a blanket – not, it would seem, out of respect, but rather because it must have been a convenient way of getting the body into the bin. Of all the ways that there are to dispose of a corpse, this was one of the most callous, disrespectful, and hurtful to those left behind and also, from the killers' point of view, the most inept. It was sure to be found fairly quickly. The girls hadn't tried to weight the bin down to ensure that it would sink. Furthermore, the water was not more than three feet deep, at most. It remained there – in full view – until the following Sunday, when police divers would pull it out and Mrs Lilley's body would be identified by a neighbour.

The girls met two men in a pub that night and spent a 'happy evening' with them. They probably needed to get as drunk as possible, and to persuade themselves somehow that their lives were still normal. Though undoubtedly they were both heartless and depraved, it beggars belief that they could really put the events of that terrible day out of their thoughts. Though the sequence of events is not certain, we know that they 'trashed' the house: they scrawled the word 'kill' in paint; emptied knives all over the kitchen floor and then flooded it; turned the gas and all the lights on, and kicked the back door in, leaving it gaping open. They put Mrs Lilley's belongings into another bin and were later seen throwing what must have been her clothes into the canal. When asked what they were doing, they said the garments belonged to them and didn't fit any more because they were pregnant. In this orgy of reckless destruction, the only precaution they seem to have taken was to hang sheets over the windows so that passers-by would not be able to see the damage.

Lisa slept in Mrs Lilley's bed, while Sarah stayed downstairs. Night and day were no longer distinct to them, defined only by the times when they could buy more drink. In the early hours of Saturday morning they hailed a cab. They were ten to fifteen minutes' drive away from Mrs Lilley's house which, they told the driver, was their own. They flirted with him, and he heard one of them tell the other that they had to clean up the mess when they got in. They asked him whether he was married, and wanted to know when he finished his shift. He knew there was something odd about them: they were too young to own their own property and certainly too young to be showing sexual interest in a man of his age. He didn't take his concerns any further: taxi drivers aren't social workers and, in any case, had he involved himself with their welfare, it could easily have seemed as though his motives were of a predatory nature. These girls were very young, and he was a grown man. He ignored his misgivings – and their advances.

Neither Lisa nor Sarah could have been rational during this period. Both were very likely drunk most of that weekend. A normal reaction would have been to run away, or at least to lie low. They did neither. One of the young boys in the neighbourhood called to see where Mrs Lilley had gone; Lisa, leaning out of a window, told him that she was Mrs Lilley's grand-daughter ('I knew she wasn't,' he said later). 'She's nutty,' Lisa yelled. 'I'm going to kill her.' That evening, two schoolboys reluctantly accepted the girls' invitation to come into the house. They, too, asked where the old lady was, and were told, 'We've killed her.' They might have believed this: judging by the state the house was in, it was obvious something dramatic had happened and the girls were behaving as though the house was their own. Besides the mess, there were signs that they had been sniffing glue. They were spitting, and stubbing cigarettes out on the carpet. One of them (probably Lisa) then said she was only joking, and added: '. . . but I wouldn't go fishing if I were you.' Both started laughing at this, but then the other (Sarah) whispered that they shouldn't make 'what they had done' so obvious.

Sex was frequently uppermost in their minds. Maybe they were hoping their two visitors would oblige. Certainly this was the case when they locked another lad inside the house and wouldn't let him out. One of the girls made sexual advances, and then said that she would be willing to let him go if he hugged her. The boy simply wanted to leave. He also must have known that something was seriously wrong: neither of the killers were making much attempt to conceal their crime.

They somehow convinced themselves that they were 'having a good time', but in fact they were trying to obliterate the knowledge of what they had done. They must have wondered, at least fleetingly, how long they could stay in the house before someone noticed that something was radically wrong, but they evidently reached a stage where they didn't actually care. Private-ly, the thought of discovery and of some authoritative, competent adult sorting out this mess and taking them in hand must, in spite of their earlier aspirations to independence, have seemed an attractive idea.

About this time, as children will, they fell out. Perhaps they disagreed about what they were going to do next, or perhaps they were just getting on each other's nerves. They must have realised that it would be only a matter of time before they were caught. Subconsciously, they must have known that when that happened, they could no longer stand together.

It seems that on the Sunday there was a heated dispute over some matter, which left Sarah wearing only her underwear and having to demand her clothes back from Lisa. Her naïve idea, after all this had been resolved, was to go home to her mother and put all the blame onto Lisa. If she had thought this course of action through, presumably she had seen in it some slender advantage in being the first to speak: that this would register in her favour. She also knew – only too well – that the actual murder and the details of their cruelty were things that only the two girls knew about: when it came to making a statement to the police, it would be her own word against Lisa's. On the other hand, by now, she might simply have been filled with revulsion at what they had done.

When her mother heard the story, she vomited.

Lisa, meanwhile, had also gone home, but had said nothing of the events of those last few days. She surely could not have imagined that they would get away undetected, and the thought of Mrs Lilley's corpse, only half-submerged in the grimy waters of the nearby canal, must have weighed heavily on her mind. It didn't take long for a further development to occur. Police found the body, and later that day, Sunday 27 September 1998, the two girls were taken in for questioning.

They were found guilty at their trial and were sentenced to detention 'at Her Majesty's Pleasure'. In November 2002, Lord Woolf ruled that they must serve at least eight years. Their desire to run away from home had led to horrible cruelty and the death of a kind old lady. Mrs Lilley's popularity with the local youngsters was borne out by the large number of them who attended her funeral.

Lisa Healey is said by prison staff to be quiet and polite and has apologised for what she has done. Sarah Davey, on the other hand, has tried to commit suicide and is said to have 'only a limited understanding or acceptance of the gravity of the offence'.[9]

8. BLOOD BROTHERS

Just before one o'clock in the morning, on Monday 26 November 2001, firefighters were called to deal with a fire at 1104 Muscogee Road in Escambia County, Florida. Inside the house, they found the body of 40-year-old father of two Terry Lee King lying on a recliner. At first it appeared that he had been asphyxiated, but closer inspection revealed wounds to his head. The fire, which had raged in the other side of the house, seemed to have been intended to cover up the man's murder, but the killer, or killers, had not succeeded: the room where Mr King's remains were found had been untouched by the flames.

Mr King's sons – Derek, who was thirteen, and his twelve-year-old brother, Alex – were missing. King had reported their disappearance. Nobody knew whether the subsequent search for the boys was going to turn up two more bodies. There were those who suspected the two youngsters were – at the very least – heavily involved in the murder of their father.

There had already been press interest in the family: Terry King had called the *Pensacola News Journal* on Thanksgiving Day (22 November) and reported that his children had not come home since the 16th. He had last seen them on the morning of that day, when he had taken them to Ransom Middle School, where they were pupils. He felt certain that they had not run away of their own volition, as they had no extra clothing or other possessions with them when they left him. King had said that he was telephoning the paper in an attempt to get the Sheriff's office to take his concerns seriously. In fact, he was not the legal guardian of Derek and Alex since he and the boys' mother, Janet French, were not married. Janet – also known as Kelly Marino, a one-time exotic dancer – had left the family and gone to live with another man who, according to Terry King's father, used to beat her. There had been an attempt at reconciliation with King, but it hadn't worked. In 2001, she was living in Kentucky and the boys saw her so rarely that Derek in particular, had he met her, would not have known who she was.

Only four days before the children disappeared, King had withdrawn them from school.* They had informed their teachers that this was because they were going to visit their mother in Kentucky. The very morning before he called the paper to enlist its help in tracing them, King had asked for their names to be put back on the register. They had attended that particular school for less than twelve months; it seems that their educational history, like their home life, had been chequered.

None of their neighbours had known the family at Muscogee Road very well. Derek and Alex were the kind of good-looking, clean-cut, 'All American' boys one might expect to see in a film about high-school romance. The Kings had moved to this address the previous summer, but had not forged any close links with the local community: they had 'kept themselves to themselves'.

---

* This conflicts with his statement that he had dropped them off at Ransom on the 16th: the day they disappeared. However, both versions are documented in various reports and so we must assume King had his own reasons for saying they were meant to attend school on that day.

Derek had returned home only a few weeks before he and his brother disappeared. Since coming back to live with his father, he had shown his dislike of the rural isolation in which he found himself. Before that, he'd spent six years in the care of religious foster-parents. The couple had finally decided that they had done all they could for this difficult child. The subsequent move back 'home' came as a blow. He had always suffered from attention-deficit hyperactivity disorder and he had a temper, but he was well liked by his former school friends and, to all outward appearances, had been a 'normal kid'. The trouble was that he was a normal kid in a sense, but he hadn't been given a normal childhood.

A 'family friend', 40-year-old Rick Chavis, was interviewed after the fire and criticised Terry's handling of his two sons. He maintained that King was a 'control freak', whose over-strict disciplining of the two young boys had alienated them completely.

The boys' mother, Janet, hotly contested this view of her former partner's parenting skills. She had been with Terry for eight years before their relationship broke down in 1992, although she continued living in the same house as her ex-lover for another two years after that. At that time, the family had also included Janet's twin sons by another man. Unfortunately, financial pressures had become too great: King's meagre wages from his work in a variety of printing shops around the area had not been sufficient for them to live a comfortable life.

When they heard about the Heritage Christian Academy, a 'crisis home' for young children, it seemed like the answer to their problems. The Academy (which has since closed down) was run by the Rev. Steve Zepp, who readily agreed to look after the four children while their parents sorted out their affairs.

After eight months, Mr Zepp suggested a more satisfactory solution. This was 'open adoption', whereby the children would go to live with foster families but always have access to their natural mother and father. He told Janet that sometimes the best thing to do for children was to give them up. What was proposed seemed like a good idea to the parents but, though none of the adults involved were doing anything short of their best, the two children were growing up with the impression that they were nothing but a nuisance to the people they needed most: they felt that they were being passed around like unwanted pets. Janet has since expressed her hurt at the implied criticism that she has been subjected to from several quarters. She loved her children and, though the last thing she wanted was to let them go, she genuinely didn't know what else to do: 'I know a lot of people are saying stuff, but it hurt me, and we had to do what was best for our children. Those people aren't in my shoes. They don't understand how hard it is to care for four boys under those conditions.'[1]

Young Alex hated being away from home and cried all the time. Within a month, it had become clear that he could not be happy where he was and he was allowed to go back to his parents. However, his twin stepbrothers seemed content, and it seemed as if Derek was going to benefit from the care of Frank and Nancy Lay, with whom he lived, as it happened, for the next six years.

Frank Lay was the principal of Pace High School. He and his wife were keen Christians and Derek became a popular and helpful member of the Olive Baptist Church where Mr Lay was a deacon. As has been said, Derek certainly had a temper, which used to flare up every now and then – particularly when someone criticised his natural family. However, he was apparently responding positively to an upbringing that at last provided him with boundaries and a structured life. A minister at the church said that Derek had 'a scarred heart'[2] and that it wasn't surprising that he was a bit rebellious. Another official said that Derek was 'a little boy with a tough package of emotions who'd gone through some things that no little boy should have to go through'.[3] Other members, as well as some school friends, remember his sense of fun, his energy and his off-the-wall sense of humour, as when he prepared eggs without the aid of a whisk: he simply put them in a bag and shook them up.

His teachers remember a capable, bright child who was an average to above average scholar. They had had some minor disciplinary problems with the boy, but nothing out of the ordinary. He always tried his best to be courteous, and involved himself with sports and other activities. The coach of the amateur basketball team he was with considered him to be a 'sweet kid' who was in 'good hands' with the Lays.

This is not the story that came out later, however. Frank and Nancy Lay testified in court that Derek had always been trouble. Though they admitted that his life with them had begun well enough, they became alarmed when they discovered his preoccupation with fire. They had dealt with this by forbidding him to have matches, and might have thought that he was over his fixation had not their worries been renewed when he refilled a kerosene container with gasoline: it was fortunate that he didn't have the means to ignite it. Nancy Lay described the boy as 'a perpetual conman'.[4] 'He was always in and out of trouble,' she said. 'Probably just about every rule we put down he broke at one time or another.' It transpired that the reason for Derek being sent back to live with his father was that the Lays had decided to send him to military school and Terry had objected to this. After he had returned home and subsequently run away again, taking Alex with him, Mrs Lay and her husband had, by chance, come across the brothers. Derek had told her that he didn't want to go back home. He told her that he and his brother were going to kill their father. 'We already have a plan,' he said.

Meanwhile Alex had apparently been getting most of his education directly from his father. Terry was working at a printing company in Pace, doing the 2 a.m. to 10 a.m. shift. The boy would spend his nights in the lunch room at the print works, where he idled the time away by reading Harry Potter books, playing on his 'Game Boy', colouring, or sleeping on two chairs he pulled together for the purpose. His father was able to keep an intermittent watch on him and he was kept out of the way of the other workers. Another employee, John Carroll, couldn't see any serious difficulty in this situation: '[it] worked because he was such a well-behaved kid,' he said. When Derek came out of foster care in October 2001, Terry King took both boys to his workplace. Yet his boss commented, 'That situation was never a problem. I just assumed it's kind of hard, being a single dad, to find a day-care centre open at night, so I let it slide.'[5]

There are two very different versions of the relationship between Alex and his father. In one Alex King was, like his elder brother, a happy child with a good sense of humour. He, too, liked to play practical jokes: he would ring the telephone operator and, when the call was answered, burp into the phone. According to this account, none of his extended family had any inkling that there was trouble brewing. In the other version – the one Alex himself provided in his statements to the police – Terry was a strict disciplinarian, who used to 'stare him down'. Alex had been subjected to physical abuse from his father – with a belt and a switch or stick of some kind – and felt brow-beaten, driven to seek a means of escape from Terry. That escape came in the dubious form of 40-year-old 'family friend' Rick Marvin Chavis who, Alex said, had become his lover.

Chavis, an auto mechanic and air-conditioning repair man who was ostensibly friendly with Terry King, already had a conviction from 1984, when he was sentenced to six months' imprisonment for molesting three teenage boys. He was a paedophile whose influence on the two young brothers can only be described as unsavoury; but to them he was an adult friend, who didn't care about the imposition of rules, or morals, or discipline. His house – a well-known 'hang-out' for the local youngsters – became a refuge where Derek and Alex were able to watch TV (there wasn't one at home), smoke marijuana and play computer games. Alex, on the cusp of finding out about his homosexuality and growing up surrounded by all the bilious homophobic attitudes which attend traditional Christianity, was more than willing to embrace Chavis's questionable friendship. At this point in his life, he could be said to have crossed the Rubicon. On one side was his budding sexuality and on the other the knowledge that his father, his family – and practically everyone else he knew – would condemn him for the direction that it was taking. If he sought help, the likelihood was that nobody would understand, and to compound matters he would certainly be separated from the man he had grown to dote upon.

His infatuation with this man was a childish one, but with a big difference to a normal 'crush': whereas pre-teenagers sometimes do become emotionally attached to much older boys – or even adults – it is rare that the more mature party is willing to reciprocate the kind of interest shown by the younger one. Whether Chavis actually did use Alex for sexual gratification is, at the time of writing, still under debate: he is due to be tried for the crime of assaulting Alex. Alex himself (though he does not view the alleged encounters as abuse) claims that things of that nature certainly went on. He wrote a 'diary', a series of scribbled notes illustrated with naïve drawings of hearts and ornate crosses, decorated with their initials. In it, he writes over and over that he loves Rich Chavis 'so so much and always will'. Had they not been born of the infatuation between a ten-year-old boy and a forty-year-old paedophile, these doodles might be viewed with a knowing smile. As it is, they indicate an adult's sinister manipulation of a young boy's emerging sexual awareness.

Derek seemed to be aware of his younger brother's sexual leanings and, unusually for his age, didn't appear to object to them in the slightest. According to his statements, he was protective of his brother and was getting increasingly angry at his father's treatment of both of them. The following is an edited version of his interview with the police, following his arrest:

    Derek: . . . I told Alex, if, if stuff gets serious, I will defend you.

Investigator Terry Lee Kilgore: OK. What would make you say that? Why would you say that?

Derek: 'Cos Alex told me he, he was weak and he didn't have enough, he didn't have strength to fight him off . . . fight my father off.

Investigator John Sanderson: Did you feel like they might, something might happen? I mean that's what he's talking about why y'all were having that conversation.

Derek: Why, because we . . . 'cos we were scared that something might, since we, he . . . that was the day he got both of us back. Um, I was . . . I was just afraid that once he got both of us back he would get physical with both of us . . . both of us at once.

After their arrest Wilbur King, their grandfather, told how the brothers became violent towards each other in front of him. He inferred from this that they had always had that tendency, but he was not necessarily correct. He then asked Alex exactly what had happened on the night of Terry's death. Before Alex could answer, Derek put his finger up to his lips, telling him to keep quiet. Alex instantly obeyed, and the subject was dropped.

During another visit, Derek told his grandfather that the Olive Baptist Church was prejudiced: they were against homosexuality. He asked his grandfather if he, too, was against it and, predictably, the old man said indeed he was: 'It's dirty. It's filthy and the Bible is against it.' This was precisely the reaction that Alex had been doing his best to avoid. His older brother must have known this, and may even have taken the same view as his grandfather. By this time, Mr King was aware that Alex was declaring himself to be gay, but no doubt blamed this on Chavis's malign influence. He put the question 'Are you a homosexual?' to the older boy. Derek threw his arms up above his head as though to protect himself from the thought. 'No', he said. 'I'm not.'

On 24 November, the deputy Sheriff of Santa Rosa County found Derek King in a wood near Pace. Alex's statements to investigators John Sanderson and Terry Kilgore described what happened. In them, he narrated how he waited for Derek in the woods. Derek had gone to make a phone call and was away such a long time that Alex eventually concluded (correctly) that he must have been caught. After spending the night in the wood, not knowing what to do, Alex called Chavis, who came and picked him up. They went to a fast-food restaurant to get something to eat and to wait for Terry King, whom Chavis had telephoned. After a while, Terry arrived with Derek. The investigator interrupted at this point and, to clarify, asked if the 'Terry' referred to was Alex's father. Alex replied: 'But biologically he is not my dad. He's not my father – biologically.' The investigator passed over this remark and asked what they did next. While Terry had been buying food, he and Derek, Alex replied, had briefly 'been talking a little bit about the matter of their father dying'. This possibility wasn't anything more than a vague notion at that point. Alex was worried about what was going to happen to them when they got back home and to kill their father seemed to be a possible way out of their difficulties. After it had been mentioned, the brothers went on to talk about cars (they hadn't discussed which of them might carry out the murder). If Terry was the disciplinarian that they alleged him to be, it seems odd that, as Alex tells the investigating officer, he and his brother were 'horseplaying' for some time just after discussing the murder. This was surely not the way two terrified boys would behave with an angry father who was about to beat them only a few feet away.

Terry, he went on to say, had taken them home eventually. Derek had gone into his room to play, while Terry had questioned Alex about his reason for running away:

Alex: So, then . . . I noticed that Terry was in the green room. I went in there and then, well, he called me in there and . . . he started asking why I ran away and I was saying because of what happened.

Kilgore: And what happened?

Alex: Well, the day that we ran away, before we went to the – to the school . . . he threw us around . . . we couldn't take it anymore because . . . he had done that before . . .

Kilgore: OK. Now you talk about he's done it before – I mean what do you talk about him doing?

Alex: Abuse.

Kilgore: Well, what type?

Alex: Mental and physical.

Kilgore: OK.

Alex: Mental. He was staring us down every time we got in trouble. He was using, um, extreme eye contact.[6]

He said this 'extreme eye contact' was not something that affected him any more since he had managed to become 'pretty strong in that aspect', but that Terry also used to hit them.

Alex: Well, he hit me a couple of times. It wasn't very often that he did, but he hit me a couple of times with the back of his hand: well, basically slapped me across the face.

Kilgore: OK. Well, let me ask you this, the times that he'd slap you across the face and you say that he didn't do it much, was it because you were in trouble, or something had happened or what?

Alex: Well . . .

Kilgore: Were you being disciplined?

Alex: No. He was, um, he must have had a bad day and I just . . . I was talking and he hit me and told me to shut up . . . a couple of times. I think that was all the times he hit me. Wasn't very often.[7]

He then said that a 'long time ago' his father once used a stick on him. He 'couldn't recollect' what sort of stick it was since he was very young then. Most times, he claimed, Terry used a belt. Apparently contradicting what he'd just said about not being hit very often, he went on to say that he'd been in trouble 'so many times'. He'd been whipped with the belt 'quite a few times': 'I think it was like ten or twenty times. Once,' he said, 'pretty recently.'

Soon, what had begun as a quiet talk with his concerned father developed into a confrontation. Terry grabbed Alex by the wrist and threw him to the ground. Alex's arm hit something – he couldn't recollect what, but the impact made a mark that he still had after his arrest. He ran away and went to the room he shared with his brother at the front of the house. He told Derek what had happened and said he wished their father were dead:

I said that. I said I wished he was dead and . . . I don't
know who said it, but . . . one of us said . . . "why don't
we kill him?" . . . I said – you know – we need
something to stun him . . . the knife might not penetrate
the first time and . . . I said we could use a hammer . . .
We went back to the work table which was at the back
of the house.

They couldn't find a hammer, so they chose to use a
baseball bat. They went back to the 'green room' where
Terry was sleeping on his recliner. Alex believed he was
only pretending to be asleep, since it hadn't been long
since he'd left him and he knew that it usually took his
father some time to nod off. Derek then hit him with the
baseball bat:

Alex: It sounds about like wood cracking or . . .
  hitting concrete or something. Then he misses the
  second time and he hits the lamp . . . turns it off
  . . . and the third time the bat makes contact with
  his head. Blood comes from it and he keeps hitting
  with it. Then, um, we run, we run from the room.
Kilgore: OK. What are you doing when Derek's
  hitting him with the bat?
Alex: I was just standing there watching him.

He went on to describe the injuries in more detail:

Then he smashed – he smashed his face in. His skull –
well normally, his skull, it uh . . . His forehead is in line
. . . well, his nose comes out further than his forehead
normally . . . and he knocks a hole in his head. It's
smashed to the right . . . he hits him and the bat makes
contact with the left side and, uh, makes contact with

the forehead, knocks a hole in the forehead, you could see his brains.

With their father dead, his killers became 'kind of panicky'. They ran back into the bedroom and, at Derek's instigation, set fire to the bed. 'It was an old house and it burns easily,' said Alex. 'We knew this . . . we decided to do that because . . . it would destroy the evidence and we were real, real worried about getting caught and everything.'

He went back to describing the attack on Terry in more detail:

The noise he made the first . . . the noise he made: the first impact was a groan and he squeezed his eyes shut. You could tell that he was in pain and he [Derek] missed the second time. The third when he . . . the second time he made contact which was the third time he swung, I think it knocked him out. But the fourth time he swung: the third time he made contact, the blood came from his forehead so I knew he was out. By the time he got done he was still trying to breathe and made – sort of – like a sound like the person has a slightly stopped-up nose: made that sort of a sound. And every time he breathed out, well, the times I saw . . . his face, the skin on his face sort of puffed out from the air.'

The investigator asked if the fire had been started because they thought Terry wasn't actually dead. 'It was obvious that he was dead,' Alex replied, adding, 'Well, not dead but, 'cos of the way he was breathing, we didn't know if he was dead or not. But I knew he was already there, he had to be there, 'cos a little bit of his brains was on the wall, I believe.'

'How do you feel about that?' the investigator asked.

'Very disturbed and very scared', Alex said. 'And so we set the house on fire.'

The brothers then went to a local coffee bar where Rick Chavis picked them up. He allowed them to go to his house and shower. Asked if Chavis had known what was going to happen that night, Alex told the officer, 'I don't think he knew anything beforehand. He said that he felt that it might come down to this, but we didn't tell him about it beforehand. After what's happened a couple of days, then he knew about it because we didn't contact him . . .' His answer then became slightly garbled and the officer had to press the point: '. . . I'm talking about as far as the death of your father: did Rick know before it was gonna happen that it was gonna happen?' Alex replied, 'He didn't know for a fact but he had a feeling that it would.'

Asked how he felt now about his father's death, he said he felt a little sad but also a little relieved that he wouldn't have to go through the abuse any more. He went on: 'I feel kind of down about it. Because of the fact that – you know – it was a death and I saw it and it's just kind of real disturbing.'

The investigation into Terry King's murder resulted in three arrests and two incompatible prosecutions. In an unprecedented move, the Florida District Attorney's office tried Ricky Chavis and the King brothers for the same crime, separately and with conflicting hypotheses. When they were arrested, Alex and Derek had at first admitted to being responsible, but had since changed their story. The defence put forward at their trial was that Chavis had killed their father while they were hiding in the boot of his car. Chavis had then persuaded them to confess. He had told them that, as they were juveniles, they would be able to get away without punishment. This, then, made the case against Chavis. If it was the truth, then the prosecution's case in the second trial (presented by the same man, David Rimmer), could not also have been correct: that the two boys had killed their father and that Chavis (though no pillar of society), was not a murderer after all. The verdict from the first trial (Chavis's) had been kept in a sealed envelope and was not revealed until after the second trial. The second jury believed the boys to be culpable of second-degree murder; that is, they believed they had been responsible inasmuch as they admitted Chavis into the house, with the certain knowledge that he intended to murder their father. When the first verdict was announced, it revealed that the first jury had acquitted Chavis, thereby incriminating the boys by default. Thus two mutually exclusive theories were, at one and the same time, argued by the self-same legal system. In both cases, justice was surely compromised by a disregard for the legal requirement of 'beyond reasonable doubt'. If there was an alternative explanation of the evidence available – one that was persuasive enough to warrant a prosecution, as the system supposed – then, surely, 'reasonable doubt' must have been demonstrable in each case, and, as a matter of simple logic, neither case could be certain.

King's death may well have been the result of Derek's rage breaking out and finding the most convenient target. He was a boy who had needed help for most of his life, but what he had been given was restraint. It would have been only a matter of time before he began to resent the rigid frame his spirit was forced into; especially as the adults who demanded his obedience always seemed to desert him in the end. Chavis was stimulating, entertaining and nothing like the straight-laced adults who surrounded him. In a different environment, one without the many strictures that the boy had to endure, this man would not have had the magnetic appeal that he seems to have possessed.

Many people will see a correlation between homosexuality in general, Chavis's taste for young boys and Terry Lee King's murder. In supporting these conclusions, they will ignore the restrictive and (for Alex) damaging influence of the Christian right wing: they will, in fact, be confusing gay sexuality with paedophilia. There is a popular fallacy that lesbians and gay men have no sexual feelings until they are of an age to do something about them legally. The truth is that a gay person's emotional and sexual awakening happens in much the same way as that of a straight person and requires a similar degree of positive guidance. Alex, like so many others, found something in himself that he was led to believe was anathema to God, to his family and to the world around him. The only adult who seemed to accept him was a man whose motives could hardly be described as responsible, positive or genuinely caring. Whether or not it is true that his father beat him, or was over-strict in other ways, one thing is certain: Alex knew his father did not understand him and that there would be little point in trying to persuade him to see things differently. Alex was caught in the middle of two opposing forces and was left with a choice between hating himself or hating his father. If the verdict was correct, he chose to hate his father.

On 17 October 2002 Judge Frank Bell, of Escambia County Circuit Court, ruled that the prosecution's presentation of two different explanations for the crime amounted to a violation of the boys' rights to due process of law. He ordered that the prosecution and defence must try to resolve the case in mediation. If they were not able to do so, and should the prosecution's appeal against his decision fail, then he would order a retrial.

'There's no question in my mind, based upon legal arguments and trial transcripts, that Derek and Alex King did not receive due process,' he said. Legal experts who agreed with him were doubtful of justice being achieved by a retrial and interpreted the order of mediation to suggest that the judge agreed with them in this. Prosecutor David Rimmer said he trusted the original verdict but refused to comment any further.

The brothers were present when Judge Bell announced his decision. They smiled and Alex laid his head on the table in front of him. However, they will remain in custody at Escambia County Jail until the final resolution has been reached. Their defence lawyers are hopeful of avoiding the need for another trial. 'This gives me a great deal of hope,' one said of the decision. 'I'm hoping mediation for both sides goes well.' Another claimed to be 'ecstatic'.

Should his ruling be overturned following a prosecution appeal, Judge Bell will officially sentence both boys.

In February 2003 (which will be after this book has gone to press), Chavis is due to stand trial on charges of lewd and lascivious acts upon a minor; he intends to plead not guilty. In November, the boys pleaded guilty to third-degree murder. They will avoid the longer sentences they faced as a result of the original trial verdict. Alex will serve seven years in prison and Derek, eight years.

9. BLOOD LUST

'How do I know if I'm a vampire?' This, strangely enough, is one of the frequently asked questions on vampire websites, which are many in number and range from the obviously facetious, through sociological studies, to pseudo-religious cults whose members would answer such a question with complete seriousness. Apparently, the most common indications of an individual having a 'vampiric' nature are: a preference for nocturnal activity; a hyper-sensitivity to any kind of light; a blood fetish, including a craving to drink blood; a need (and the ability) to absorb the energy of other living beings; a 'profound desire' to be a vampire; a knowledge that you are radically different from 'ordinary' people; and, finally, some or all of these coupled with a pre-existing or emergent auto-immunity.

For those who have wondered why they find fulfilment in having their lover pierce their flesh in order to draw blood; and for those who feel a need to do this to others, help is at hand. There are people who will not condemn the craving as unnatural but who will understand it, and who will welcome the worried, fledgling vampire into their fraternity: 'We're just a bunch of people who happen to be vampires ... We have lives, not un-lives, and we'd like to keep it that way.'[1]

The Vampire/Donor Alliance's website – www.darksites.com – will seem rather 'weird and wonderful' to most people, but it does at least explain vampirism in terms that render it a relatively harmless activity. It describes a vampire as a person who lacks energy and therefore needs to draw extra life-force into their system from some source other than mere metabolism after eating a conventional type of food. Some of the practices by which one can achieve this include: standing against a tree, and allowing its power to seep into you; standing in a crowded room (at a party or nightclub, perhaps) and letting the communal vitality wash over you; eating foods rich in 'prana' (a Hindu word having a meaning akin to 'life-force') such as raw fruit and vegetables, eggs, yoghurt, cheese and fresh milk (it is recommended that the latter be got direct from the cow, in order to achieve the desired effect of sating one's craving for blood); 'red' drinks are best, and lots of them – and, of course, there's always a good old rare steak. Oddly enough, this isn't high on the list of recommendations: the writer advises that steak juices are mainly water and food colouring, but admits that it can be beneficial as a placebo.

All this is not to say, though, that modern vampires don't feed off each other's blood. The people who are willing to take a passive role in this activity are called 'donors' and they're in demand. For the most part, it's a consensual practice between people who are aware of the potential dangers and who take sensible precautions. Although it may seem bizarre to the rest of us, vampirism is, like sado-masochism, a variant way of expressing sexual and (in the case of the former) spiritual feelings. The Vampire/Donor website includes health warnings and such unequivocal comments as '. . . the "drain and resurrect" technique is pure fiction, so if you are entertaining the thought of being "turned" that way, forget it. It is true that a near-death experience can often catalyse an inner streak of vampirism, but actual death will only kill you.'[2] Most of all, the site does not subscribe to the myth that drinking another person's blood will result in immortality, or even prolong life.

It may be controversial to say that being a vampire is only dangerous when the concept is fed into an impressionable, incautious mind but, as is the case with witchcraft, this comment would appear to be true.

In the summer of 2002, a teenager from the Welsh town 'with the long name' Llanfairpwllgwyngyll-lgogerychwyrndrobwillllantysiliogogogoch (Llanfairpwll for short) became the subject of sensational newspaper reports after he was found guilty of murdering one of his elderly female neighbours with, it appeared, the sole intention of feeding from her blood in order to gain immortality. Matthew Hardman was seventeen and he had steeped himself in vampire lore for some time.

He was the son of Paul and Julie Hardman, a bricklayer and a nurse. His childhood was nothing out of the ordinary, and was spent on the Welsh island of Anglesey, where he was a poor to average attainer at the local primary school. If there was, in his history, any emotional trauma that might have been a contributing cause of his unnatural proclivities, it came when his adored father and mother decided to separate when he was only eight years old. His mother moved in with her boyfriend, a fireman for the Ministry of Defence and, like many children of divorcees, Matthew spent time at both his parents' homes. His retiring nature meant that he didn't mix well with others. This was noted when he moved to Amlwch High School, but was ascribed to the fact that he suffered from dyslexia. He was given extra tuition, which proved an embarrassment for him when his fellow pupils found out about it; but his good manners, coupled with his natural reticence, did endear him to the adults he knew, though it made it difficult for him to relate to others of his own age.

Paul Hardman died young; his son was fourteen – an age when to be robbed of a father can create deep emotional scars. Matthew moved in with his mother in Caernarfon, but after three changes of address, the family eventually found themselves in Llanfairpwll. Matthew was still isolated and withdrawn, but initially appeared to be a reasonably normal lad. He earned pocket money from a newspaper round. One of the houses he delivered to belonged to an elderly, rich widow, Mrs Mabel Leyshon. She had lived in Llan-fairpwll since just after the death of her husband in the late 1950s, in a bungalow that had been built specially for her. She was well known locally as a sharp-tongued, traditional kind of old lady who could sometimes be brusque with people she didn't know. She discouraged strangers from visiting her house, and would be short with those who did call unannounced.

Matthew was becoming 'difficult'. He had an obsession with death and killing; he was acquiring a reputation at school for being a 'weirdo'. Children who are different from others often have to suffer the taunts of their classmates and he was frequently picked on. His only friends were exchange students from abroad who, no doubt, were sufficiently vulnerable themselves to ignore his eccentricities. He collected knives and kept a replica Magnum that he displayed on his bedroom wall. He listened to depressing 'death metal' music and liked to draw ghoulish sketches of decapitations and of victims of torture being disembowelled. When he left school and began studies at art college, he took a keen interest in the paintings of the Mexican artist Frida Kahlo.

Kahlo has been perceived by the art establishment as a surrealist, but she herself discounted this label when she said, 'I never painted dreams. I painted my own reality.' She had polio as a child, which left her with a limp. In her late teens, the bus on which she was travelling crashed into a tram. She suffered further injuries to her right leg and pelvis and the accident left her unable to have children. Her paintings were to reflect the cruel hand that fate had dealt her. Her life was always controversial: for example, she had an affair with Trotsky, and was also friendly with the man who assassinated him.

In 1955, just before her death, gangrene forced her to have her right leg amputated; it was rumoured she may have committed suicide.

Kahloism is a bizarre cult that holds Frida Kahlo to be the one true deity and her friends – including her husband, Diego Rivera – also to be deities beneath her. It is debatable whether this 'religion' is genuinely believed (it is also debatable whether it could be said to be a religion at all). More likely, in keeping with its tenets, it was founded on a deliberate attempt to shock. Though the 'vampire movement' has no direct connection with Kahloism, Kahloists would no doubt approve of it; in fact they go to great lengths to assert their individuality. Besides having to keep a shrine to Frida in his or her room, a Kahloist must celebrate the significant events in her life by 'doing something really cool'. In this fraternity, discovering oneself to be a vampire would certainly be regarded as 'cool'.

Matthew had left school and found employment as a part-time porter at a local hotel. He was smoking cannabis regularly – not in itself a worrying trait – and was not only delving into Kahloism, but had also persuaded himself that he was a vampire. One of the magazines he read described a mock interview with a vampire and gave instructions on the way to dismember a corpse and prepare it for eating later. His beliefs were not benevolent in the slightest: he wanted to live forever and would do anything to achieve this. He held that he could achieve immortality by drinking human blood and letting others drink his own.

On one occasion he attempted to turn himself into a willing 'victim'. He asked a sixteen-year-old German student, Anna Hassler, to bite him on the neck, apparently thinking that this would be his rite of passage into the world of the 'undead'. Ms Hassler was one of the exchange students he had befriended. She lodged with one of Matthew's few friends and willingly allowed him into her room one night when he turned up asking if he could chat with her. The conversation lasted for some hours and revolved around Matthew's macabre interests. He told her that Llanfairpwll was a perfect place for vampires because of the high proportion of elderly people who, if they were bitten and subsequently died, would be presumed to have perished from a heart attack. Ms Hassler was, not surprisingly, appalled when he told her that he knew she was a vampire and could help him to be one also. It would be quite easy, he told her: all she had to do was to bite him on the neck. When she refused, he grew violent. He pressed his neck against her mouth and begged her to do as he asked. At this, she screamed for help. Her cries brought others to the scene; Matthew also accused each of them of being a vampire. He proceeded to hit himself on the nose, apparently thinking that the blood would prove irresistible to them. When the police arrived, as he was being handcuffed, Matthew asked the officer to bite his neck.

It is possibly – even likely – that drugs and drink could have induced this behaviour. It could, equally well, have been a terrible confusion of sexual desire and morbid fascination. Whatever the case, Matthew's arrest did not discourage his dark fantasies: two months later he resolved to undergo initiation as a vampire, come what may.

Mrs Leyshon had already had minor confrontations with Matthew, during his time as her paperboy. He had several times left her garden gate open, and she had reminded him to close it. She was herself an artist, but preferred tasteful landscapes to the avant-garde works Matthew admired. She had her gentle eccentricities, such as placing teddy bears at strategic points around the house to serve as reminders to switch off the immersion heater or to do various chores. Otherwise, she was a perfectly ordinary old lady: exactly the type of elderly person that Matthew had described to the German student. She had no children or close family and followed a mostly solitary lifestyle. If she had ever crossed Matthew sufficiently to merit hatred, he never referred to any such occasion and it would seem that she was simply an ideal candidate for his first foray into practical satanic ritual. The date of her death, Saturday 24 November 2001, coincided with the eve of the death of Frida Kahlo's husband and was therefore one of the 'holy' days marked by Kahloists for 'doing something really cool'.

Matthew half-planned what he was about to do, but must have realised, had he thought about it, that he would be suspected almost immediately. If he cared about this, he cared only as far as to take the precaution of putting on gloves before he broke into her neatly kept bungalow. He then crept up on her as she sat watching television. The sound was turned to high because of her deafness and the old lady didn't stir from her chair when Matthew broke the glass in the back door with the aid of a slate from her garden. He was carrying a six-inch knife that he'd taken from his mother's kitchen.

A 'Meals on Wheels' worker found the body the next day. Mrs Leyshon had been stabbed 22 times: twice through her heart. Her stockings had been removed and her legs propped up to allow her blood to drain through the gashes in her legs. A saucepan, placed in a ritualistic manner on a silver platter, bore the culprit's lip-print where he had drunk the 'life fluid'. He had ripped her heart out, wrapped it in newspaper and put it into the saucepan. The room had at some stage been arranged for a black magic rite: a candle had been lit on the mantelpiece and two pokers formed the shape of a cross on the hearthrug. Matthew Hardman was now a vampire.

The shocked town was told that the maniac who had done this might well strike again. The police had two major clues: DNA from the gory lip marks; and a footprint – the killer had been wearing trainers – that had been left on the slate used to break into the house.

Two days later, police making door-to-door enquiries questioned Matthew. He claimed that he'd been at a friend's house on the night in question. When the details of the murder became public, among the two hundred phone calls received, two referred to local gossip about a boy who had asked friends to bite him on the neck. Matthew's room was searched and its contents left little doubt as to the nature of his fantasies. The knife, still showing traces of Mrs Leyshon's blood;

a recently-washed trainer that matched the footprint, and the DNA, all confirmed his guilt. When he was arrested, he turned to his mother and said, 'Don't worry, it's all right, Mum –I didn't do anything'.[3] After three days of questioning, when asked if there was anything he wanted, he asked the officers if they would get him a Big Mac and French fries.

He always maintained his innocence and, throughout the initial period following his arrest, betrayed no emotion whatsoever. He told the police that he couldn't remember much about the night in question because he'd been too 'stoned' on cannabis, and said that his vampire fetish was merely a 'subtle interest'.

In court, his personality changed somewhat. He was nervous; his face twitched; he was breathing deeply and he wrung his hands frequently. His mother attended every day of his trial at Mold Crown Court. When, after three and a half hours' deliberation, the jury returned a unanimous guilty verdict, the judge, Mr Justice Richards, told him: 'I am drawn to the conclusion that vampirism had become a near obsession with you. You really did believe that this myth may be true and that you would achieve immortality by the drinking of another person's blood. One might hope for a psycho-logical explanation for your behaviour but none is available. You hoped for immortality. All you achieved was to brutally end another person's life and bring a life sentence upon yourself.'[4]

As he was led away in tears, his mother mouthed to him, 'I love you.'

10. NO ANGELS

The following 999 call* was placed in the afternoon of 27 November 2000.

> *1st Caller:* Can you send an ambulance to Blakes Road . . . it's a boy bleeding to death: he's actually bleeding to death.
>
> *2nd Caller: (who has taken the phone)* This boy is approximately twelve years of age. He has lost a hell of a lot of blood.
>
> *Operator:* How has he done that? What happened?
>
> *2nd Caller:* We do not know, sir. We have just come out and found him on the staircase.
>
> *Operator:* Where is he bleeding from?
>
> *2nd Caller:* We cannot tell.
>
> *Operator:* Have a look to see what part of his body is bleeding.
>
> *2nd Caller:* Actually it looks like it's coming from his leg.
>
> *Operator:* Is it the upper leg?
>
> *2nd Caller:* It looks like from the upper leg; shall we raise his leg?
>
> *Operator:* No, don't move him.
>
> *2nd Caller: (to his friend)* Don't move him! Don't move him!
>
> *Operator:* Is he awake? Is he conscious?

---

* This transcript has been edited.

2nd Caller: No, it looks like he's drifting off.

Operator: Is he conscious?

2nd Caller: No.

Operator: Is he breathing?

2nd Caller: Is he still breathing? Is he still breathing? He's still breathing.

Operator: Can you get a clean cloth or a towel? Is he awake at all?

2nd Caller: No, it looks like he's going unconscious. Is he still with us?

Operator: Speak to him. Try and bring him round . . . Sir, can you go to where the patient is please?

2nd Caller: I am with him right now.

Operator: Get a coat over his body to keep him warm.

2nd Caller: We got that; we got that.

Operator: Is he breathing normally?

2nd Caller: He's breathing, but he's . . .

Operator: Is he making any noises as he is breathing?

2nd Caller: No, he's very quiet.

Operator: Is the blood squirting out?

2nd Caller: He's actually wearing trousers and the blood seems to be coming from underneath his leg.

Operator: Is there anything you can cut the trousers with? You are going to have to do it. . . . Is there a lot of blood?

2nd Caller: There is a hell of a lot . . . He is still breathing but he is in a very bad way.

Operator: I want you to check that he is still breathing.

2nd Caller: Is he still breathing? Keep checking him; keep him talking. Try to keep him talking. Is he

awake? Keep him talking. Try and get him to talk
to us. We need to cut the trousers . . . nice and
carefully.

Operator: Have you got something to put on it yet?

2nd Caller: We've got some gauze.

Operator: You are going to have to stem the
bleeding.

2nd Caller: We still can't see the cut . . . this could
be a stomach wound. It looks like it could be the
stomach. It's coming down his trousers.
(*He tells his friend to lift up the boy's top*) It might
hurt him a little bit but we're gonna have to.
It's from his leg. Right, we've found it.

Operator: Can you place the gauze on the wound?
Can you manage to do that?

2nd Caller: We think that is the wound but to be
honest, he's stopped bleeding.

Operator: Can you see any blood pumping?

2nd Caller: Keep him going. Keep him going.

Operator: Is he awake?

2nd Caller: No, he keeps drifting off: He's . . . .The
police have just arrived.

Operator: Has he stopped breathing now?

2nd Caller: He's just checking. They're actually
trying to check now. No pulse, no pulse.
(*One of the police officers that have come onto the
scene takes the phone:*)

Operator: Has the patient stopped breathing?

Police Officer: Yeah, apparently so.

Operator: Right. OK, do you know how to do
resus?

Police Officer: We will try to get on it.

Operator: Right. He's definitely not breathing?

Police Officer: Jim, is he definitely not breathing?

He's definitely stopped breathing.

Operator: Try and get one of your hands under his neck, put one on his forehead and pull his head back slightly.

Police Officer: Jim, Jim . . . we need one hand behind his neck, tilt his back about an inch. Open his airway. Look in his mouth to see if there is anything blocking his airway. Obstructions, Jim. Pinch his nose tight and breathe two deep breaths into his lungs. Cover his mouth completely. Jim.

OK. He's doing that.

Operator: Have you located the wound yet?

Police Officer: Yes, we've located wounds on his legs.

Operator: Is the breath going in? Is his chest rising as you are doing it?

Police Officer: Is the chest rising?

Hold on a sec . . . no, the chest is not rising.

Operator: You need to check if there is anything in his airway.

Police Officer: Jim, put your fingers in – put your fingers in.

He's going to stick his fingers in and find out. His tongue's up: there's nothing blocking it.

Operator: OK. Try once more. Cover his mouth completely. Remember to pinch his nose closed. Is his chest rising?

Police Officer: Yeah, it's rising.

Operator: OK. What I want you to do now is feel for a pulse.

Police Officer: I'm doing it. I can't feel a pulse . . .[1]

The boy, ten-year-old Damilola Taylor, died in hospital within an hour of a vicious attack that had left him with a gaping wound in his leg. One of the men who had found him, a carpenter called Guillermo Casal, told in court how he had later seen a youth – one of three standing near to where the boy had been found – drawing a hand across his leg in a mimed imitation of the fatal injury. Mr Casal wept as he described Damilola's last few moments of life.

He had parked his van near an office block in Blakes Road on the North Peckham Estate in south-east London. Then he had noticed what he took to be a squashed tomato on the pavement but soon realised that it was blood. He followed its trail up two flights of stairs leading into a block of flats. There, he found Damilola was in great pain after having staggered 30 yards towards his home – he was only 200 yards from it when Mr Casal found him.

There was a large blob of blood with a footprint in it. I saw the boy standing up four or five steps. He was holding his shoulder against the wall. He just looked at me and I looked at him and I just ran to the boy. He fell down. I rushed over to him and crouched down by him. There was blood everywhere. I asked him what had happened; where he was bleeding from. The first thing he said was: 'I'm OK. OK.' I didn't hear him say anything else. I told him he was not OK and he began to collapse into semi-consciousness.[2]

Mr Casal dialled 999 on his mobile telephone and ran to fetch some of his colleagues. Three men responded and, though they did everything the operator instructed, they were unable to keep Damilola conscious. Police arrived but their efforts to resuscitate him were also in vain. It was not until the post-mortem examination that the reason for this was discovered: a glass marble had been forced down the boy's throat. It ensured that, if he didn't bleed to death first, he would almost certainly choke before any professional help could reach him.

Damilola had only been in Britain for three months. The family had moved to London from Nigeria so that his adult sister could receive medical treatment that was unavailable to her in Nigeria. They had moved onto the North Peckham Estate where they lived with other relatives. Damilola had enrolled at the Oliver Goldsmith Primary School where he was known to be always smiling and never disrespectful. He made friends there and joined a computer club at Peckham Library, which he attended most days after school. The only cloud on the horizon was that, as a new pupil, he was a victim of bullying at school.

CCTV cameras, which have so often witnessed the prelude to these tragedies, show Damilola walking home from his computer class at 3.46 on 27 November. He is wearing his large, silver 'puffa' jacket and appears to be in good spirits. The following description of the attack is what was alleged in court. It has never been proved and, since the spectacular collapse of the trial, probably never will be.

Damilola was confronted by a group of youths: not an unusual occurrence on this type of estate. Here was a vulnerable little boy who might well be carrying valuables – a mobile phone, money, it really didn't matter – in fact Damilola had little to interest a thief other than his trendy jacket.

Possibly angered by having wasted their time on a boy who wasn't worth robbing, one of the gang fetched a beer bottle from a nearby rubbish area. He broke it and handed it to one of his friends. Within moments, the other boy had stabbed Damilola in the thigh and had twisted the glass into the flesh because this, he knew, would keep the wound open. The bottle had severed a major artery and vein, causing profuse bleeding. Damilola was jumping up and down in pain, and to shut him up, one of the boys forced 'a marble or something'[3] down his throat.

The gang then fled, leaving Damilola to almost certain death.

The four boys who were indicted for the murder of Damilola were no strangers to trouble. Two of them, twin brothers aged fifteen, had been responsible for a mini-crimewave involving drugs, intimidation, sexual harassment and worse. They came not from the North Peckham Estate where crime was the order of the day for so many young residents, but from a more pleasant part of Peckham where they lived in a flat which had a garden; their mother cared for them and worked extremely hard to give them the best possible chance in life. She refused to believe that her children had been involved in something as terrible as murder, admitting that they were 'tearaways' but saying they could never hurt a little boy. 'I know they're no angels but . . .' – it's a phrase that has been trotted out by so many incredulous mothers expressing their complete faith in their children's innocence. In this instance, as in almost every other, it was an understatement made in the defence of two out-and-out thugs who had terrorised their neighbourhood for most of their young lives. What drove them to become so unruly is not quite clear: there appear to have been no obvious signs of deprivation apart from the fact that their father left the family when the boys were two years old. Their other brother and two sisters managed to complete their education and go on to college or to start their own families without getting into trouble. It would be easy – and perhaps comforting – to simply believe that these two boys were 'trouble'.

In November 1999, the brothers, fourteen at the time, were with three others when they saw two girls in a local park. The girls – ten and twelve years old respectively – were subjected to an attack that was to leave them psychologically damaged for years to come. The boys forced them to the ground and tore away their clothes. Thinking they were about to be raped, the girls screamed for help. Luckily the mother of the twelve-year-old was on the other side of the park and ran to their rescue, causing the boys to run away. As they did so, one of them shouted 'You'll never get us!'

On these 'sink' estates the 'immunity' of young delinquents is well known to be exploited by older criminals – particularly by drug dealers – who use them as 'safe' couriers of crack cocaine or as handlers of stolen goods. If they are caught, their age means that no meaningful prosecution can result. Safe in the knowledge that all they have to fear is a ticking-off, the youngsters reoffend with impunity; they laugh in the face of anyone who tries to stop them, to reason with them or make them see the error of their ways.

In another sex attack, a fifteen-year-old girl described how she and her friend were stripped naked and assaulted by the same group of thugs. When she reported the incident to the police, she was subjected to a campaign of harassment. The boys gleefully shouted the same phrase to her: 'You can't touch us, we're untouchables!'

Their mother worked as a shop assistant during the day and in a restaurant in the evening. She had also taken cleaning jobs – a neighbour described her as 'the most hard-working person you're likely to meet'.[4] The woman described how the mother arrived at her flat one day with her hands 'red-raw'. When the neighbour commented, the mother simply laughed it off, saying she'd been working too hard.

At school the behaviour of the two brothers was bad from the moment they started. As small children, they threw stones at people, and by their early teenage years they were unmanageable.

So many inner-city estates have become wastelands: empty shops; boarded windows; litter-strewn streets; graffiti and gangs of surly, aggressive teenagers. These are youths (male and female) that society does not know what to do with. They have grown up outside the system and feel themselves to be at war with the world. They are frequently dealing in and taking drugs from very young ages and have, like boys A and B (as the courts knew the brothers), been excluded from school.

The people of Peckham have made great strides to improve its image and have, with constructive initiatives and recent developments, to some extent succeeded in bringing hope to the area. However, the teenagers who rule the dark, deserted streets after nightfall are unlikely to be helped by any community project. The leader of a local youth project has described them as 'kamikaze kids'. She says they have, like suicide bombers, nothing to lose and care nothing for the feelings of others or for the environment in which they live. She estimates there are about a thousand of them in Peckham, all at a serious stage of moral disintegration and most without any thought to their own future; the predictions are that they will probably live lives blighted by drug addiction, prison and violence.[5]

Boys C and D, too, had a background of violence. Boy C had already been an inmate of the notorious Feltham Young Offenders' Institution in West London at the time he stood trial for the attack on Damilola; he seemed to take the possibility of returning there completely in his stride. At seventeen when he came to trial he was the oldest of the four. He, like Damilola, had only been in Britain for a short time – a few years in his case – having come over from Africa with his mother and two sisters, leaving his father back at home. In the winter of 2000, only a day after they were bailed following their arrest for Damilola's murder, Boys C and D were allegedly involved in an assault on one Mustafa Das who was set upon in Burgess Park, Peckham. Five youths surrounded him, demanded cash and threw a metal barrier at his head, causing a cut that needed 30 stitches. Boys C and D were cleared of this assault because of lack of evidence. In October 2002, Boy C and another friend of his were suspected of being involved in an arson attack on a builder's yard in Peckham. They claimed they had climbed into the yard to relieve themselves, which is why they were outside the builder's cabin when it exploded. The judge agreed with them that it couldn't be proved that they had anything to do with the fire and they were once again set free because of insufficient evidence.

Boy D, who was thirteen in 2000, was thought to be less criminally active than his cohorts. He came from a one-parent family where his mother, who drank heavily, had had children by several different men. It was Boy D who had spoken against hurting Damilola: when Boy C had said, 'I'm going to juke this boy' ('juke' being a slang word for 'stab'), Boy D had said, 'No, leave him.' His defence maintained that he had also suggested calling an ambulance. He was 'deeply damaged' and may not have been able to understand what was being said in court.

The *Daily Express* described the police investigation as 'long and exhaustive' and told how the defendants, together with other youths, had been arrested 'several times'. In fact, from the very beginning, proof of the case against them was sketchy to say the least. Defence counsel Baroness Mallalieu QC claimed that the police had simply rounded up 'the usual suspects': all four boys were known troublemakers and the police had set about manufacturing the case against them because of public pressure.

However, while their guilt was hard to prove, they could hardly claim to be unfairly suspected: whilst being held for other crimes at a young offenders' institution, they had allegedly talked about Damilola's death. One of the brothers had told another inmate that they had decided to steal the boy's puffa jacket; another had supposedly confessed to his intention to rob Damilola of any money he might be carrying. According to the inmate, they had said, 'Damilola would not give up what we wanted so we cut him.' Prosecuting, Mark Dennis said:

> In what can only have been a deliberate and controlled act of violence, Damilola was stabbed as he remained trapped and helpless, surrounded by all four boys. As he cried out and jumped up and down with pain, one of the gang placed a glass marble into his mouth. The stabbing caused a deep and gaping wound which severed a main artery and vein and caused immediate and profuse bleeding . . . The explanations given for the final violence were somewhat chilling – to one youth it was said it had been done for laugh, to another that it

*had been done because Damilola had ignored them, to
another that he had been 'getting mouthy'.*

He later told the jury: 'This was an act of violence
which, you may think, had been committed by those
without compassion and with a hard and cruel streak in
them.'[6]

Given their dreadful past, their obnoxious personalities
and the horrible crime that had been committed, most of
the newspaper-reading public would have, no doubt,
been glad to see these young people 'get what they
deserved'. One of the boys was reported as having said he
thought the killing 'rather funny'; another wrote a poem,
found by police at his house, which began 'I went mad
when I heard he was ten. But never fuck around with me';
in the young offenders' institution, one of the brothers had
allegedly boasted that they were going to get away with it.
He had told another boy that the police had nothing on
them; his mother had burnt his clothes, he said, thereby
destroying any evidence they might have found.

Court 12 of the Old Bailey had been specially adapted
for the trial. After criticisms of the way Robert Thompson and Jon Venables were handled after the murder
of James Bulger, the authorities went to even greater
lengths to ensure that the young defendants would not
be intimidated by their surroundings. To this end, the
formal lines of furniture were moved into a semi-circle;
a limited number of media representatives were allowed
into the court and it was they who were seated in what
had been the dock, whereas the accused sat in the well
of the court where they could see everything properly.
The court kept to regular hours with frequent breaks
and whenever the boys were moved about the building,
the corridors were cleared so they didn't feel they were

being stared at. Those who took charge of them didn't wear uniforms and the judge and barristers put aside their wigs and gowns. Writing in the London *Evening Standard* after the trial had ended, Paul Cheston said that the idea that the sight of wigs and gowns would intimidate these hardened criminals was 'frankly laughable'. However, it was undoubtedly done in the interests of justice and in order to make sure that the accused were given an absolutely fair hearing. In the event, the trial turned out to be a complete fiasco.

It began on Wednesday 30 January 2002 and was presided over by Mr Justice Hooper. Evidence was heard from Guillermo Casal, the carpenter who had first found Damilola. He brushed away tears as he told how he had followed the trail of blood to where the little boy was standing, supporting himself against a wall. He told how Damilola had tried to tell him he was 'OK' and how he, his colleagues and the police had fought to save his life. He described the youth who had made the 'cutting motion' across his leg but admitted that that boy was not one of those present in the court.

The case for the prosecution began to break down when they produced their 'star' witness, a fourteen-year-old girl codenamed 'Bromley', who gave evidence from behind a screen. She told the court how she had been in Peckham at the time of the murder and how she had seen three boys she knew – the two brothers, Boy C and another boy who was unknown to her – running into Blakes Road. She had followed them because she was 'being nosy', and described the events that followed:

I thought they were talking . . . then I saw them moving their hands and I thought they were robbing someone: a little boy. I saw them passing a bottle. I think they were

237

saying something to the little boy . . . then they just hit him I think.

They were all standing around him in a circle . . . one of them walked round the corner to a dump, I think, and came back. He had something in his hand. I didn't know what it was at first. They began passing the bottle around. Then one of them hit him with the thing then they all started to run.

The brothers were standing in front of him, the other two boys were standing beside him. They were just turned around and were looking out to see if anyone was there. I was behind a car.

I was going to run after them. But I thought I might as well go home. I did not think I would catch up with them because they were running.

[Damilola] was saying, 'Help'. He got robbed and I didn't want to go up to him because I might have got into trouble for this.[7]

Muggings, she said, were common in Peckham and it was 'not unusual for the brothers and them lot to rob people'. She claimed her decision to speak out had followed an attack of conscience: when she realised the police were arresting innocent people it was, she said, 'time to do something about it'.

She later told the court, 'If I had a brother and that had happened to him, I will need someone to come forward. They were arresting people that were not there and I knew [the accused were]. I called *Crimestopppers* but their line was engaged.'[8]

It became evident almost immediately that her evidence could not be relied upon. She was consistently antagonistic towards the defence and resented almost every question put to her.

Mr Courtenay Griffiths QC, representing Boy A, accused her of having made up her dubious account. She admitted she had lied to the police when they had first questioned her but Mr Griffiths pointed out that her final version of the story was also doubtful. For one thing, she couldn't remember where she was standing when she witnessed the attack. 'The reason you cannot remember is that you were not there,' Mr Griffiths said. He concluded that her tale was 'complete nonsense'; that she had made up her evidence because she craved attention and because she thought she would 'look incredibly brave and important'. Bromley displayed her true colours immediately.

'For one, I'm not a liar,' she shouted. '. . . You may think that I am [a] liar . . . [but] no matter how many times you try to catch me out you are not going to catch me out, because I am not a liar.'

Mr Griffiths replied: 'Which police officer gave you that little speech to repeat?'

'No police officer,' she snapped. 'I'm not answering you. I don't like the way you're talking to me. You're talking to me like I'm a little girl.' Mr Griffiths said that, at fourteen, she was indeed a little girl. She replied: 'If you talk to me like that, I'll talk to you like a little boy.'[9]

She then began answering the barrister's questions in a sarcastic voice with the words: 'I can't remember', after which she asked to go home. The trial was adjourned for the day.

The next day (5 February) she halted proceedings for a second time. Mr Griffiths put it to her that she was still telling untruths. 'Do you know what?' she replied. 'I haven't got time for you. For one, I'm not a liar. For two, you're trying to wind me up. Well you've got there. Are you happy now that you've wound me up? You have wound me up; do you like it? You don't like it when I ask you questions . . .'[10]

The judge explained to her that Mr Griffiths was not allowed to answer her and she calmed down for a short time. Then the barrister asked her if another piece of her story was merely a figment of her imagination and she lost her temper again: 'It wasn't my imagination. It's your fucking imagination. I want to go home now . . . I'm not playing with this man.'[11]

She was evidently aware of her status as the chief witness for the prosecution and, like some temperamental actress, had decided she was too important to have her performance spoiled by incidental players. Mr Griffiths asked her to look at photos of the area. She didn't want to. 'You know what?' she said. 'I'm going home.' With that she stormed out of the witness box and left the courtroom.

An hour and forty minutes later, she returned, explaining in an injured voice that Mr Griffiths had upset her. A few minutes later, annoyed by further questioning, she was again asking to go home. 'He keeps upsetting me,' she said. 'He keeps on doing it and he knows that he is doing it.'[12] The judge tried to reason with her, saying: 'This is a very important case and the defendants are entitled to ask questions through their barristers. It's my task to ensure that they are fair. Once or twice I have corrected Mr Griffiths . . . the best thing for you to do is to remain calm.'[13] She rested her elbow on the side of the witness box and graciously agreed to continue.

Mr Griffiths questioned the veracity of her first call to the police. He suggested she had merely repeated details that she had either picked up from the television and newspapers or heard from other people.

She had already admitted that some of her original statement was untrue; she had explained this away by saying she was afraid of being implicated because she might have found herself in trouble. The judge asked her if she wished to stay in the court while the jury heard recordings of her interviews with the police. Tearfully, she replied that 'no,' she didn't. She wanted to go home.

Her reliability as a witness fell apart completely when it emerged that she fully expected to claim the £50,000 reward that a newspaper had offered for information leading to a conviction. George Carter-Stephenson QC, defending one of the brothers, played some of the nine hours of videotaped interviews she had had with PC Carolyn Crooks. Mr Carter-Stephenson told the jury to be aware of her references to the reward. On the tape, left alone with the teacher who was standing as the required 'responsible adult', Bromley told her: 'I don't get none of this money until I'm eighteen.'

'What money?' the teacher replied. 'You ain't even telling them nothing yet.'

Later, Bromley told the woman, 'I'm going to Spain for free.'

'Oh yeah?' the teacher said. 'So how come you're going to Spain for free?'

' 'Cos the police are paying for it,' she replied.[14]

The prosecution tried to paper over the cracks by pointing out that the reward had been offered three days after the killing and the girl had taken three whole weeks to come forward – surely a bounty hunter would have been quicker off the mark. The argument was weak and he must have known it.

The whole treatment of Bromley was woeful. Even the teacher wasn't as 'responsible' as might have been wished: told she might be required to stay for a further two hours, she complained, 'You've got to be kidding . . . I'm getting bored.'[15]

Bromley's rapaciousness was more than clear but, as if to underline it, she was caught on camera singing 'I'm in the money' and, making a grasping motion with her hand, saying 'gimme, gimme, gimme, gimme'.

Prior to the trial, Bromley and her mother (who had convictions for drug dealing) were housed at the Selsdon Park Hotel in Surrey. The cost of this should have been £79 a night for bed, breakfast and dinner. The bill rocketed as the pair made free with the facilities. They made hundreds of telephone calls – on one day there were 60, including one costing £246.40. Bromley explained that she had been bored and had wanted to speak to her friends. A day's bill for alcohol came to £58 for one room and £33 for the other; food, extra to the set meals, came to £74 on one day. Within seven nights the bill for one room had escalated to £2,090 and for the other to £2,040.

'You have been taking people for a complete ride, haven't you?' Baroness Mallalieu said.

'No, I haven't,' Bromley replied peevishly '. . . I am stuck in a hotel and I am not allowed to go out into the world.'[16]

The week's stay at Selsdon Park ended when she was asked to leave in the middle of the night after setting fire to her room. She and her mother were moved to a flat, the cost of which was £1,341.98 per week. The police gave her a mobile telephone – she sold it. PC Crooks lent her a Sony Walkman – she sold that too. At one point she became so drunk she had to be taken to hospital.

Boy C was the first of the defendants to be acquitted. With Bromley's evidence completely discredited, the judge ruled that he had no case to answer. Speaking of Bromley's 'performance', he said: '. . . no part of her evidence which is adverse to any defendant can be relied on.' He went on to say that she had a fertile imagination and had repeatedly embellished her story. She had, he pointed out, confessed to lying in her statement and had admitted exaggerating 'to make the story sound good'.

'No jury,' Mr Justice Hooper said, 'could be sure that she was telling the truth about anything important.'[17]

The three remaining boys weren't off the hook yet. The rest of the case against the brothers was made up of witness statements testifying that they had 'confessed' to the crime whilst being held at Feltham Young Offenders' Institution on an unrelated matter and, more vaguely, that the attitude of one of them at the time of his arrest was defiant and provocative.

The dilemma the prosecution had to deal with was that the boys were likely suspects – the most likely – but it was simply not going to be possible to prove it. Boy A said he had been at his 'godsister's home' [sic] in another south London borough at the time of the attack. Workers at a care home who had seen him near the murder scene within an hour of the stabbing disputed this. The pair had also allegedly been overheard inventing an alibi. It was said that over thirty inmates at Feltham Young Offenders' Institution were willing to testify that they had bragged about their involvement; in the event most of them were thought too unreliable to be called. One who *was* called claimed one of the brothers had told him how he had stuffed a marble in Damilola's mouth to stop his cries of pain:

We were talking in the showers . . . He told me what happened. He told me he was there but he didn't do nothing. There was five of them. They saw [Damilola] walk past and they called him over. The boy didn't have any money and someone said, 'You must have fifty pence.' He told me one of them's got a knife. One of them stabbed him in his leg. I can't remember the name. He told me the boy was jumping up and down in pain. To shut him up they put something in his mouth – a marble or something.[18]

Another witness from Feltham, an eighteen-year-old trainee professional footballer, said, 'He seemed happy for what he had done. He said the reason why he had killed him was because he was mouthy. He was getting too lippy.' The youth, who had been at the institution for robbery, said one of the accused had told him they had mugged Damilola and robbed him of a mobile phone before killing him – Damilola didn't have a mobile phone.

Two teenagers came forward to testify against Boy D. One said he had confessed to killing Damilola; it had happened after a joke went wrong. He [the witness] had called the television programme *Crimestoppers* after he had seen news items about the trial.

Other, equally unreliable, 'confessions' were reported: that the gang had killed Damilola 'for a laugh'; that he had been murdered because of his African accent – the stories may well have been told by the accused boys or they may have been entirely fictitious; some could have described part or parts of the truth but none could be relied upon absolutely. In cross-examination, a witness who had testified against Boy D admitted that he too had attacked a ten-year-old boy at knife point. He had told the child: 'Give us your money or we will slit your belly open.'[19] He readily admitted to committing countless robberies and at least 150 burglaries, and confessed to being addicted to drugs. Psychologists confirmed that he craved attention and that he was likely to fabricate stories and exaggerate in order to get it.

The other witness against Boy D had been a heroin addict since the age of twelve. He took delight in seeing others get into trouble.

More reliable testimony against the two brothers came from a prison officer, Darren De'ath, who told how he had asked a group of inmates if any had committed grave crimes that would warrant long sentences. One of the brothers had laughingly replied he had: 'possibly murder'. An inmate asked him who he'd murdered; the other brother said: 'Damilola Taylor – but we didn't kill him. We just stabbed him in the legs. It was not our fault that he died.' Later De'ath asked if what they had said was true. He said they had laughed and he quoted them as saying: 'Just hypothetically speaking but we are not telling you any more because you are just interested in the £50,000 reward.'[20]

This should have been a more concrete piece of evidence; it was given by a man who at least had more credibility than the young felons who, expert liars to a man, might well have sold their grandmothers in the hope of special treatment at their own trials. Unfortunately, Mr De'ath undermined the reliability of his story when he was cross-examined. He said that it was entirely possible that the boys had said what they did in order to appear tough in front of the others and so avoid bullying.

Boy D was the next to be acquitted, almost a month after Boy C. The judge, after consulting with the barristers, said that, having considered the case against him very carefully, he had decided the only proper verdict was one of not guilty. The boy did not react as the charges against him were formally dropped but the two brothers wept openly.

At the beginning of April, with their case looking increasingly shaky, the prosecution had to combat evidence from accident surgeon Alistair Wilson who, in total disagreement to their own expert witness, claimed Damilola might not have been stabbed after all but that his fatal injury might have been the result of a fall.

Crucial defence evidence came from the fact that, seven minutes after the stabbing, calls had been made from the two teenagers' mobile phones. They had been traced to Bermondsey, which is over two miles from Peckham.

On 25 April 2000 the jury returned a unanimous verdict of 'not guilty'. The boys burst into tears in front of the assembled court. Damilola's father bowed his head despairingly and his mother looked stunned. It was the fifty-fifth day of a trial that had cost an estimated ten million pounds.

It is, of course, impossible to say whether or not any of these unpleasant young men were responsible for the crime: the words of Boy A, sadly and ironically, turned out to be all too pertinent: 'Prove I was there. Prove I was there that day. Can you prove I was there at the death?'[21] With a lack of forensic evidence, a succession of unreliable witnesses and disputed 'confessions', it would never be possible to bring a solid case. It was as an article by Anthony Scrivener QC in the London *Evening Standard* was headed: 'The Trial That Should Never Have Happened'.[22] However, it must be pointed out that, although the onus was not upon them to prove their clients' innocence, the defence presented evidence that was also equivocal. If, as their expert witness claimed, Damilola had simply fallen on a broken bottle, how did he come to have a glass marble in his throat? Bromley and the inmates of Feltham may well have been lying; they could equally have been telling the truth. After dismissing the cases against Boy C and Boy D, the judge directed the jury to acquit Boys A and B if they believed the calls made from Bermondsey had come from telephones that did indeed belong to them. He maintained that they couldn't have covered the distance in the time; yet *Evening Standard* reporter Chris Millar who was, as he put it: 'an unfit twenty-seven-year-old, keener on sessions in the pub than in the gym' was able to cover the distance in six minutes thirty seconds by using a short-cut across Burgess Park.[23]

There was also prosecution evidence that the judge had ruled inadmissible before it officially came to court: such as that of social worker Anne McMorris, who visited Boy A at Feltham. In the absence of the jury, she described him as having been in a state of 'extreme distress'. He had told her: 'We stabbed him. We didn't mean to kill him.'[24] She admitted, however, that his emotional condition meant the statement could not be relied upon and the judge decided his words did not constitute a confession. However, it seems unlikely that a boy who was inventing stories about being involved in a murder in order to appear 'tough' would subsequently use the same tale when he was looking and feeling anything but.

In October 2002, the stairwell where Damilola was found bleeding to death was demolished. At the time of writing, work has begun on the building of new homes as part of the £280 million regeneration of the area. The project is scheduled for completion by the beginning of 2004.

The Leader of Southwark Council, Councillor Nick Stanton, commented: 'Of course the demolition is tinged with sadness and we cannot help but remember the terrible events of two years ago.

'But it also marks a new beginning for people who have been living in terrible conditions for too long. Thousands of people in Peckham are enjoying the new homes that have been built over the last seven years and soon there will be even more.'[25]

The Damilola Taylor Centre was reopened in July 2002 after being refurbished. A sculpture of a phoenix, designed in his memory, stands in the grounds of the Oliver Goldsmith Primary School.

CONCLUSION

Recent cases of children being brought to court on charges of homicide still appear weekly: on 5 February 2002 in Point Clare, thirty miles north of Sydney, a boy of fourteen pleaded guilty to killing a three-year-old girl after abducting her as she slept. She was found stabbed to death in January 2001; her body was only yards from her family's house.

On 12 June, two youths were found guilty of stabbing another youth to death and were sentenced to a total of eighteen years in prison. The incident had happened after a drugs deal went wrong: James Petegrino, who was seventeen, was fatally stabbed on the Grahame Park Estate in Colindale, London, after agreeing to sell cannabis to Delroy Joseph. Petegrino and a group of his friends were approached by Joseph and his co-defendant, Michael Morris. The newcomers asked to buy drugs. Joseph and Petegrino moved to a secluded corridor where, after some negotiation, a deal was struck. An argument developed and eventually Joseph left the scene on his bike with Petegrino in pursuit. The two youths came to blows. Joseph was heard shouting: 'Get the borer' (street slang for a knife) and 'stab him'.

In Warrington, Cheshire, on 5 July 2002: a teenager was charged with the murder of a 75-year-old retired engineer, who was stabbed at his home on 29 May. The widower died of his wounds three days later. A fifteen-year-old local boy was charged with his murder and burglary.

Brief reports from hundreds; they are increasingly easy to find. One might take the impression that childhood is now a thing of the past; that teenagers have no respect for others and most cannot hope to become useful citizens; that the streets will never be safe again and that our world is getting sicker and sicker. None of this is true: if it were, these cases would not warrant a mention in the papers, much as punishment beatings in Northern Ireland have ceased to become news simply because they happen so frequently.

People have different experiences of childhood and different reactions to it. Some people may only have memories of long, happy summers, of loving families and close friends, but not the majority of us. Similarly, the horrors experienced by Mary Bell are thankfully rare. However, children whose lives have been tainted by drugs, violence, prostitution and homelessness are increasingly prevalent. Dispirited, chronically addicted and resentful, they are now an accepted part of every city and are evident even in affluent areas. We no longer flinch when we see youngsters begging on the streets or sleeping in doorways. Few of them will go on to kill but many represent a genuine threat to the rest of us: these are young people who feel they have no investment in a society that has done nothing but reject them.

Children who commit grave crimes must live with the consequences of their actions for many years to come. Though, tragically, their victims also suffer for the rest of their lives (if they survive), we must always consider the youth of the culprit and his or her ability to comprehend the full gravity of the offence. None of us would like to have indelible stains on our character, especially one formed when we didn't know any better. Which of us could look back on our childhood or our teenage years and say we were utterly responsible and hold by everything we did and said?

Tim Bateman, a spokesman for the National Association for the Care and Resettlement of Offenders (NACRO), says: 'Some forms of delinquency, which would involve breaking the law, are relatively routine and common among teenagers. It's part of growing up and probably always has been. At that kind of level there's nothing unusual about young people who break the law other than, by and large, most of them are boys as opposed to girls.'[1]

With adult killers there is usually an accepted duty to make an example of the offender as well as to eventually rehabilitate him or her into society; with children the need to look at causes and seek ways to alleviate problems and to heal psychological wounds will usually outweigh the punitive function of the law. Of course, a child who has killed is likely to remain in official custody for a number of years and eventually there comes the time when, no longer juvenile, they must either be released or serve time in an adult prison. Like a fugitive from justice who returns from exile to face the music, the grown-up delinquent finds little sympathy in the public attitude. Even when it is deemed acceptable to release them before prison can do its inevitable damage, there are those who believe 'once a killer, always a killer', and the ex-offender must live in secret, always fearing that he might be unmasked. In June 2002 new sentencing guidelines were brought into play. European rulings set the minimum sentence for juvenile killers at four years and took away the right of politicians to set 'tariffs' over the decision of a trial judge.

Needless to say, this provoked controversy. In July, the *Mail* carried a double page article that outlined the terrible crimes of 46 'cold-eyed young killers'. The implication was clear: none of them could possibly have reformed and would continue to represent a danger to society unless they stayed locked up. Such an argument neglects to take into account the fact that all of them would have to be released at some stage and, as in the case of Robert Thompson and Jon Venables, the decision to keep them away from the destructive environment of prison, and to help them learn to be better people, was surely a wise one. By this, I do not intend in any way to ignore the terrible pain of those who have lost loved ones through these appalling acts of violence, but understanding why and how these crimes come about is always an option worth exploring.

We must also acknowledge the responsibility we have as parents or adults. A child's understanding owes much to what it sees around it and it will imitate what it understands to be the way 'grown-ups' behave. I recently witnessed a harassed mother walking down the high street pushing her baby in an overladen pram and dragging a toddler by the hand. The little boy was struggling to keep up at the same time as he was demolishing an ice cream, most of which was ending down his front. Then the top fell off the cornet and landed with a splat on the pavement, splashing the shoe of a man at a bus stop. The man smiled and began searching for a tissue. Ignoring him (or maybe it was partly for his benefit), the woman landed her son a mighty whack across the back of the head and began yelling at him: 'Now look what you've gone and done! You happy now? Are you? ARE YOU?'

As soon as she had started this tirade, she stopped. Sounding tired rather than angry, she told her son to get a move on. The little boy stopped his tears instantly and, seemingly without a care in the world, they went on their way. Further up the road, she hit him again (I couldn't see or hear what he'd done this time). He kicked her leg and ran on ahead with her still yelling at him but not, it seemed, with any expectation that he was listening. When he turned his face in my direction I could see he was laughing.

He was learning.

NOTES

Introduction
1. Marr, John, *Murder Can Be Fun* #17.

2. As Time Goes By
1. All quotations in this chapter: *Murder Can Be Fun*, op cit, except:
2. The *Chester Chronicle*, August 1863.
3. Ibid.
4. Ibid.
5. Ibid.

3. The Boy Who Loved Poisons
1. Graham Young's 'diary' as quoted in *Obsessive Poisoner* (see below for details).
2. Young, Winifred, *Obsessive Poisoner* (London, Hale, 1973).
3. Ibid.
4. Ibid.

4. The World's Worst
1. Sereny, Gitta, *Cries Unheard* (London, MacMillan, 1998).
2. Ibid.
3. Ibid.
4. *Cries Unheard*, op cit.
5. Sereny, Gitta, *The Case of Mary Bell* (London, Pimlico, 1995).

6. *Cries Unheard*, op cit.
7. Ibid.
8. Ibid.
9. Ibid.
10. *The Case of Mary Bell*, op cit.
11. Ibid.
12. Ibid.
13. *Cries Unheard*, op cit.
14. Ibid.
15. Ibid.
16. Ibid.
17. Kelly, Stan, 'Liverpool Lullaby'.
18. *Cries Unheard*, op cit.
19. Ibid.
20. Ibid.

5. The Killing of James Bulger

1. Thomas, Mark, *Every Mother's Nightmare* (London, Pan Books, 1993).
2. Smith, David James, *The Sleep of Reason* (London, Arrow, 1994).
3. *Every Mother's Nightmare*, op cit.
4. Ibid.
5. Ibid.
6. Witness statement.
7. *Every Mother's Nightmare*, op cit.
8. Ibid.
9. Ibid.
10. Ibid.
11. Police interview tapes.
12. Ibid.
13. Ibid.
14. *Every Mother's Nightmare*, op cit.

6. Murder on Hungerford Bridge
1. Police interview tapes.
2. Ibid.
3. Witness statement.
4. BBC Television.
5. Police interview tapes.

7. The Body in the Canal
1. Vox pop by author on streets of Oldham, June 2002.
2. *Evening Chronicle*, Oldham, 28/07/99.
3. Telephone interview with the author, July 2002.
4. *Evening Chronicle*, Oldham, 14/07/99.
5. Interview with the author, June 2002.
6. Ibid.
7. *Evening Chronicle*, Oldham, 16/06/99.
8. Ibid, 21/11/99.
9. *Daily Mail*, 2/11/02.

8. Blood Brothers
1. *Pensacola News Chronicle*.
2. Ibid.
3. Ibid.
4. Court reports.
5. *News Chronicle*, op cit.
6. Police interview tapes.
7. Ibid.

9. Blood Lust
1. www.darksites.com.
2. Ibid.
3. *Daily Mail*, 3/08/02.
4. *Daily Mirror*, 3/07/02.

10. No Angels
 1. The *Guardian*, 5/02/02.
 2. *The Times*, 1/02/02.
 3. The *Metro*, 9/03/02.
 4. *Evening Standard*, 25/04/02.
 5. Ibid.
 6. The *Mirror*, 31/01/02.
 7. The *Nation*, 11/02/02.
 8. Ibid.
 9. The *Guardian*, 5/02/02.
10. The *Metro*, 6/02/02.
11. The *Guardian*, 6/02/02.
12. Ibid.
13. Ibid.
14. The *Sun*, 7/02/02.
15. Ibid.
16. The *Independent*, 12/02/02.
17. *Evening Standard*, 27/02/02.
18. The *Metro*, 6/03/02.
19. *Evening Standard*, 26/04/02.
20. The *Metro*, 5/03/02.
21. *Evening Standard*, 28/02/02.
22. Ibid, 25/04/02.
23. Ibid, 26/04/02.
24. Ibid, 25/04/02.
25. London Borough of Southwark website, November 2002.

Conclusion
 1. Interview with the author.

BIBLIOGRAPHY

Cavadino, Paul, *Children Who Kill* (*treatment of juveniles in different countries*) (Waterside in association with the British Juvenile and Family Courts Society, 1996)

Gardiner, Muriel, *The Deadly Innocents* (London, Hogarth Press, 1977)

Heckel, Robert V and Shumaker, David M, *Children Who Murder: A Psychological Perspective* (Westport, Connecticut, Praeger, 2001)

Jackson, David, *Destroying The Baby In Themselves: why did the two boys kill James Bulger?* (Nottingham, Mushroom Bookshop, 1995)

Jones, Frank, *Murderous Innocents* (London, Headline, 1994)

Morrison, Blake, *As If* (London, Granta, 1997)

NACRO, *Children Who Commit Grave Crimes* (*a policy report*), April 2002

Sereny, Gitta, *The Case of Mary Bell* (London, Pimlico, 1995)

Sereny, Gitta, *Cries Unheard* (London, MacMillan, 1998)

Smith, David James, *The Sleep of Reason* (London, Arrow, 1994)

Thomas, Mark, *Every Mother's Nightmare* (London, Pan, 1993)

Wilson, Patrick, *Children Who Kill* (London, Michael Joseph, 1973)

Young, Winifred, *Obsessive Poisoner: the strange story of Graham Young* (London, Hale, 1973)

Look out for other compelling, all-new True Crime titles from Virgin Books

MY BLOODY VALENTINE – Couples Whose Sick Crimes Shocked the World
Edited by Patrick Blackden

Good-looking Canadian couple Paul Bernardo and Karla Homolka looked the epitome of young, wholesome success. No one could have guessed that they drugged, raped and murdered young women to satisfy Bernardo's deviant lusts. Nothing inspires more horror and fascination than couples possessed of a single impulse – to kill for thrills. Obsessed by and sucked into their own sick and private madness, their attraction is always fatal, their actions always desperate. The book covers a variety of notorious killer couples: from desperados Starkweather and Fugate, on whom the film *Natural Born Killers* was based, right through to Fred and Rose West, who committed unspeakable horrors in their semi-detached house in Gloucester, England. With contributions from a variety of leading true crime journalists, *My Bloody Valentine* covers both the world-famous cases and also lesser-known but equally horrifying crimes.
£7.99 ISBN: 0-7535-0647-5

DEATH CULTS – Murder, Mayhem and Mind Control
Edited by Jack Sargeant

Throughout history thousands of people have joined cults and even committed acts of atrocity in the belief they would attain power and everlasting life. From Charles Manson's 'family' of the late 1960s to the horrific Ten Commandments of God killings in Uganda in March 2000, deluded and brainwashed followers of cults and their charismatic megalomaniac leaders have been responsible for history's most shocking and bizarre killings. Jack Sargeant has compiled twelve essays featuring cults about whom very little has previously been written, such as the Russian castration sect and the bizarre Japanese Aum doomsday cult that leaked sarin gas into Tokyo's subways.
£7.99 ISBN: 0-7535-0644-0

DANGER DOWN UNDER – The Dark Side of the Australian Dream
Patrick Blackden

Australia is one of the most popular long-haul tourist destinations, but its image of a carefree, 'no worries' culture set in a landscape of stunning natural beauty tells only one side of the story. *Danger Down Under* lets you know what the tourist board won't – the dark side of the Australian dream. With a landscape that can be extremely hostile to those unfamiliar to its size and extremes, and an undying macho culture – not to mention the occasional psychotic who murders backpackers, or crazed gangs of bikers and cultists – there is much to be cautious of when venturing down under.
£7.99 ISBN 0-7535-0649-1

DIRTY CASH – Organised Crime in the Twenty First Century
David Southwell

There was once only one Mafia: now every country seems to have its own. Until fairly recently gangsters kept to their territories, but crime – like every other business – has been quick to take advantage of the new global economy. Business, it seems, is good, with over $150 billion laundered each year in Europe alone. As links are formed between the Mafia, the Triads, the Yardies, the Yakuza, the Russian Mafiya and the South American cartels, a tide of misery spreads throughout the world. The book looks in detail at the specific groups involved, the horrifying crimes they commit, and the everyday lives of their members.
£7.99 ISBN: 07535 0702 1

TEENAGE RAMPAGE – The Worldwide Youth Crime Explosion
Antonio Mendoza

Columbine High School, Colorado, spring 1999. Twelve of its schoolchildren and one teacher lay dead. Two boys have gone on a killing spree, venting their anger at their classmates before turning their guns on themselves. Cases such as Columbine are occurring with increasing regularity – and guns are not always involved. In Japan in 1998, a 13-year-old schoolboy murdered his teacher in a frenzied knife attack. What is happening in society that young people are running amok, fuelled by hatred and nihilism, with little regard for their own lives and the lives of those around them? Expert crime writer Antonio Mendoza investigates this worldwide problem and comes up with some shocking findings that call for a global rethink on how we bring up – and punish – those responsible for the worldwide teenage crimewave.
£7.99 ISBN: 0-7535-0715-3

The best in true crime from Virgin Books

How to order by mail:

Tick the box for the title/s you wish to order and complete the form overleaf. Please do not forget to include your address. Please check month of publication of later titles.

From Cradle to Grave	Joyce Eggington	0 86369 646 5	☐
Perfect Victim	C. McGuire & C. Norton	0 352 32561 5	☐
Precious Victims	Don Weber & Charles Bosworth	0 86369 598 1	☐
The Serial Killers	Colin Wilson & Donald Seaman	0 86369 615 5	☐
The Last Victim	Jason Moss	0 7535 0398 0	☐
Killers on the Loose	Antonio Mendoza	0 7535 0681 5	☐
Crossing to Kill	Simon Whitechapel	0 7535 0686 6	☐
Lone Wolf	Pan Pantziarka	0 7535 0617 3	☐
I'll Be Watching You	Richard Gallagher	0 7535 0696 3	☐
Unsolved Murders	Russell Gould	0 7535 0632 7	☐
My Bloody Valentine	Ed. Patrick Blackden	0 7535 0647 5	☐
Death Cults	Ed. Jack Sargeant	0 7535 0644 0	☐
Danger Down Under	Patrick Blackden	0 7535 0649 1	☐
Teenage Rampage	Antonio Mendoza	0 7535 0715 3	☐
Female Terror	Ann Magma	0 7535 0718 8	☐
Monsters of Death Row	Christopher Berry-Dee & Tony Brown	0 7535 0722 6	☐

Please send me the books I have ticked above.

Please enclose a cheque or postal order, made payable to Virgin Books Ltd, to the value of the books you have ordered plus postage and packing costs as follows:

UK and BFPO – £1.00 for the first book, 50p for each subsequent book.

Overseas (including Republic of Ireland) – £2.00 for the first book, £1.00 for each subsequent book.

If you would prefer to pay by VISA, ACCESS/MASTERCARD, DINERS CLUB, AMEX or SWITCH,

Please write your card number and expiry date here

Card no.

Expiry date:

Signature

Send to: Cash Sales, Virgin Books, Thames Wharf Studios, Rainville Road, London, W6 9HA

Please allow 28 days for delivery.

Name

Address

Post Code